HIDDEN HISTORY of
KENTUCKY
SOLDIERS

HIDDEN HISTORY *of*
KENTUCKY
SOLDIERS

BERRY CRAIG

Published by The History Press
Charleston, SC 29403
www.historypress.net

Copyright © 2011 by Berry Craig
All rights reserved

front and back cover: Pictures of the William Whitley House, Daniel Boone and William Whitley appear courtesy of the Kentucky Historical Societs.

First published 2011

Manufactured in the United States

ISBN 978.1.59629.996.2

Library of Congress Cataloging-in-Publication Data

Craig, Berry.
Hidden history of Kentucky soldiers / Berry Craig.
p. cm.
Includes bibliographical references.
ISBN 978-1-59629-996-2
1. Kentucky--History, Military--18th century. 2. Kentucky--History, Military--19th century. 3. Kentucky--History, Military--20th century. 4. Soldiers--Kentucky--Biography. 5. Soldiers--Kentucky--History--18th century. 6. Soldiers--Kentucky--History--19th century. 7. Soldiers--Kentucky--History--20th century. I. Title.
F451.C79 2011
976.9--dc22
2010052602

Notice: The information in this book is true and complete to the best of our knowledge. It is offered without guarantee on the part of the author or The History Press. The author and The History Press disclaim all liability in connection with the use of this book.

All rights reserved. No part of this book may be reproduced or transmitted in any form whatsoever without prior written permission from the publisher except in the case of brief quotations embodied in critical articles and reviews.

To my father, Motor Machinist's Mate First Class Berry F. Craig Jr., U.S. Navy, and late father-in-law, Master Sergeant Robert P. Hocker Jr., U.S. Army—both combat veterans of the Pacific Theater in World War II and part of what Tom Brokaw called the "Greatest Generation." Also, this book is dedicated to Ed Paxton, Karl Harrison, Jack Anderson, Preston Kennedy, Bob Sanderson and the rest of the gang at the old Paducah Sun-Democrat *in 1976, when I was a cub reporter and first wrote about some of the heroes who are in this book.*

Contents

1. The French and Indian War and the American Revolution   9
2. The War of 1812   25
3. The Texas Revolution and the Mexican-American War   37
4. Fenians and Custer's "Next-to-Last Stand" and Last Stand   53
5. To the Spanish-American War   65
6. World War I   69
7. World War II   93

Bibliography   171
About the Author   175

CHAPTER 1

THE FRENCH AND INDIAN WAR AND THE AMERICAN REVOLUTION

"IT WAS NO MERE FROLICSOME PASTIME TO THE DRIVERS"

Strictly speaking, Daniel Boone was not a soldier when he received his baptism of fire in the French and Indian War.

"He was a British army contract employee, sort of like a Halliburton employee today," said James Tomasek, a ranger at Fort Necessity National Battlefield, near Farmington, Pennsylvania.

A twenty-year-old wagon driver, Boone barely escaped with his life in the one-sided backwoods battle of July 9, 1755, that went down in history as Braddock's Defeat. General Edward M. Braddock commanded a 2,400-man column of British regulars and Virginia and North Carolina militia that was nearly wiped out by a smaller force of French and French Canadian soldiers and Native Americans at what is now Braddock and North Braddock, Pennsylvania. The adjacent communities are near Pittsburgh, the site of French-held Fort Duquesne, Braddock's objective.

The general was mortally wounded in what was also called the Battle of the Monongahela. Approximately 900 of his 1,400 soldiers engaged were listed as killed or wounded. Enemy casualties were reportedly fewer than 100.

Boone was a Pennsylvania native. But he was living with his family in the Yadkin Valley of North Carolina when he signed up for army service. He might have been seeking adventure or, at least, relief from farming, which he found tedious.

Daniel Boone. *Courtesy of the Kentucky Historical Society.*

"Boone accompanied the one hundred North Carolina troops under Captain Waddell, not as a soldier, but as a wagoner, conveying the baggage of the company," according to *The Life of Daniel Boone*, a book written by Lyman C. Draper and edited by Ted Franklin Belue. Boone's job was hardly glamorous, the book says: "It was no mere frolicsome pastime to the drivers. Their most unwearied care and patience were requisite in conducting the heavily laden baggage-wagons over hills and mountain, through streams, ravines, and quagmires."

Braddock expected to capture stonewalled, star-shaped, cannon-bristling Fort Duquesne, where the Allegheny and Monongahela Rivers converge to form the Ohio—downtown Pittsburgh today. Braddock's volunteer aide was another future famous American: Lieutenant Colonel George Washington of the Virginia militia.

From Cumberland, Maryland, Braddock's column crept northwestward. To accommodate his wheeled artillery, Braddock's engineers widened a narrow road Washington had built to Fort Necessity in 1754.

The French attacked Washington and forced him to surrender the tiny, log-walled backwoods bastion in a clearing called the Great Meadows. He gave up, coincidentally, on July 4, 1754. The French burned Fort Necessity and returned to Fort Duquesne.

Beyond Fort Necessity, Braddock blazed his own road through the dense forests and occasional clearings. To speed up the advance, he divided the

The French and Indian War and the American Revolution

column. Braddock headed the lead group of about 1,400 men, which included Boone. The rest trailed several miles behind.

The terrain forced Braddock to ford the Monongahela River twice. Shortly after the second crossing—about eight miles from Fort Duquesne—between three hundred and nine hundred French troops and Indian warriors collided with the forward British column. A small memorial park at the battle site in Braddock features a bronze statue of George Washington.

Repulsed, the French and Native Americans dashed into the woods and turned the tide. Hiding behind rocks and trees, they made short work of the redcoats, who stood up and fought European style. About 450 of Braddock's men were killed, and a like number were wounded.

Washington statue, Braddock, Pennsylvania. *Courtesy of the author.*

After Braddock fell, the British regulars panicked, and the battle became a rout. Washington and the Virginia and North Carolina militia took cover and returned fire. But they, too, were forced to withdraw with the enemy in pursuit.

Meanwhile, Boone and the other wagoners waited anxiously in the rear. Ordered not to retreat when shooting started, the wagon drivers "watched the regulars flee by them," Michael A. Lofaro wrote in *The Life and Adventures of Daniel Boone.*

Boone was about a half-mile from where the battle started, according to *Daniel Boone: The Life and Legend of an American Pioneer*, by John Mack Faragher.

"Officers hastened their companies forward, leaving a guard for the wagons. As they rushed against the stalled front, the entire army crushed together like an accordion. Chaos soon prevailed amid the rain of fire. In the rear, snipers began to take their toll."

Boone and the teamsters were ordered to stay put and hold their horses at the ready for advancing to the front.

Faragher wrote:

> *But with balls whistling past their heads, many of them cut their horses from the wagons and galloped away during the first minutes of the battle... According to Boone, he remained. Nowhere could the enemy be seen, only the bursts of their rifle fire amid the trees and the men dropping "like Leaves in Autumn," as one British officer later remembered.*

The battle lasted for almost three hours, Faragher explained. Many of the colonial troops killed or wounded were likely shot by redcoats who thought they were Indians hiding in the forest.

> *A higher proportion of the officers fell. Washington had two horses killed under him, and though balls tore through his uniform, he somehow emerged without a wound. In the rear, two officers, father and son, were shot dead while Boone held his team. Braddock attempted to organize a retreat, but the wagons now blocked passage to the rear...The Indian cries and the sight of the troops rushing past, death on their faces, finally unnerved Boone. He jumped onto his lead horse, slashed its harness free, and galloped hard for the river.*

According to Faragher, the Boone family long lamented the Battle of the Monongahela in a sad ballad:

> *Until he saw all attempts were in vain,*
> *From sighs and tears he could scarcely refrain.*
> *Poor Brittons, poor Brittons, poor Brittons remember,*
> *Although we fought hard, we were forced to surrender.*

Boone was especially lucky to evade capture, according to Lofaro. He added that Indians tortured to death a dozen redcoat captives.

Likewise, Faragher wrote that

> *Canadians and Indians quickly overran the wagons, but they did not pursue the fleeing men across the ford, for they turned to plundering the rations of*

The French and Indian War and the American Revolution

rum and other supplies, scalping the dead and rounding up the wounded, who were led back to the fort to be tortured and burned at the stake. The Battle of the Monongahela, Boone's initiation into forest warfare, was one of the bloodiest and most disastrous British defeats of the eighteenth century.

Boone evidently left the battle scene on foot and headed east to visit relatives in Exeter, Pennsylvania, his birthplace, Faragher wrote. Death almost caught up with him at a bridge over the Juniata River Gorge.

"He suddenly was confronted by a big, half-drunk Indian man standing in the center of the bridge," Faragher wrote. "'He drew knife on me,' old Boone remembered, 'flourishing it over his head, boasting that he had killed many a Long Knife, and would kill some more on his way home.'"

Boone was unarmed, evidently having lost his weapons when he fled the slaughter on the Monongahela. When the Native American lurched at Boone, he ran toward his assailant. "Using his low center of gravity to advantage, he drove his shoulder hard under the big man's ribs, lifting him off his feet, throwing him back and off the side of the bridge. He plunged forty feet to the jagged rocks below," according to Faragher.

The author said Boone was elderly when he told the story of killing the Indian to the sons of one of his longtime friends. He said the man was the first of only three Indians he ever killed, Faragher added.

To Boone, slaying a fellow human being was "nothing to crow about, certainly nothing he could repeat to his Quaker kin in Exeter, and there is no record of Boone ever telling this story to the members of his own family," Faragher explained. "'Boone had very little of the *war spirit*,' one contemporary wrote. 'He never liked to take life and always avoided it when he could.' It was an aspect of his character that the Indian haters never could understand."

After a while, Boone returned to his family in the Yadkin Valley. "The experience he acquired in Indian warfare was not lost upon him," Draper wrote. "He gained too on Braddock's campaign some glimpses of the inviting loneliness of the fertile glades of the Upper Ohio Valley."

Boone's experience included a fateful meeting with John Findley, another wagoner. Findley was an experienced frontiersman who had roamed across the Appalachians.

He thrilled Boone with tales of the Great Meadow, a true land of milk and honey he said was beyond the mountains. It was the Bluegrass region of Kentucky, which the ever-wandering Boone, accompanied by Findley, would see for himself in 1769.

The Teenage Heroine of Fort Jefferson

History barely records the story of Nancy Ann Hunter, teenage heroine of old Fort Jefferson, the site of which is next to the Mississippi River near Wickliffe, the Ballard County seat.

Kentucky historians Temple Bodley and Samuel M. Wilson suggested that had the youth lived in New England, with its plentiful printing presses and book publishers, "Nancy Ann Hunter would be celebrated in history, romance and song, and known to every school girl in the land."

While Chickasaw warriors besieged Fort Jefferson during the Revolutionary War, Hunter, fifteen, reputedly braved a gauntlet of Indian gunfire to retrieve a cow and a calf. "In the fort were many infants, likely to die for want of nourishment," Bodley and Wilson claimed in their 1928 *History of Kentucky*. "Bringing that cow into the fort meant the saving of young lives."

Not a trace remains of Fort Jefferson, a one-hundred-square-foot strongpoint with log walls that General George Rogers Clark built just below the confluence of the Ohio and Mississippi Rivers in 1780. A pair of state historical society markers on U.S. Highway 51 at the entrance to the Fort Jefferson Cross, a ninety-foot crucifix, tells about the fort.

The signs do not mention Hunter. Little else is known of the young woman. But she was among about five hundred pioneers and soldiers who defended or took refuge in the fort named for Thomas Jefferson and constructed while Kentucky was the westernmost part of Virginia.

Fort Jefferson helped protect infant America's far-western frontier. The territory across the Mississippi belonged to Spain.

"A little settlement called Clarksville grew up around the fort," said Ken Carstens, a retired Murray State University archaeologist and historian. Named for General Clark, it was the first settlement in what became the Jackson Purchase, Kentucky's westernmost region.

Carstens said Clark was not at the fort when the Chickasaws began a three-day siege on August 27, 1780. The Indians did not want the Americans on their land.

But they had an extra incentive to wipe out the intruders, Carstens said. Under a flag of truce, an American soldier had shot and wounded James Colbert, a Scotsman who lived among the Chickasaws.

Angered by such treachery, the Indians, according to a contemporary account, "gathered all their force and at Night began a tremenduous [sic] fire on the fort Advancing up from all quarters till they were Crouded [sic] very Close." The whites replied with muskets and some small cannons, forcing the attackers to retreat.

The French and Indian War and the American Revolution

While the fort's officers planned their next move, Hunter spied near the fort "but within range of the Indian guns…a cow and a young calf," Bodley wrote.

He also quoted Louisville historian Reuben T. Durrett, who claimed in an 1883 speech that Hunter dashed from the fort and led the bovines back inside as Indian bullets "whistled by and cut her clothing, herself unharmed." Carstens suspected Durrett stretched the truth a tad.

But Durrett's tale is not as tall as another one told on the heroine. In that yarn, Hunter went buffalo hunting to save the fort, whose defenders were running out of food. "Supposedly, she swam the Mississippi in her voluminous skirt, killed the buffalo on the other side and floated it back across," Carstens said.

On August 30, the Chickasaws gave up and left but not before burning the settlement's "very beautiful and large Crop of corn" and slaughtering "what few Sheep & Cows were left," according to Captain Robert George, the Fort Jefferson commander.

In June 1781, the Americans abandoned Fort Jefferson and Clarksville and scattered to New Orleans, Saint Louis, Louisville and elsewhere. Afterward, the fort and the settlement disappeared.

But during the Civil War, Union forces recognized the site's strategic importance and built a dirt-walled fort where the old log fort had stood. A third historical marker commemorates the Civil War earthwork.

The heroine of Fort Jefferson earned a few lines in other history books besides the one by Bodley and Wilson. Also, the teen was the subject of a school play performed in Murray. "Otherwise, she's a mostly unsung heroine in the region she helped settle," Carstens said.

THE HERO OF LITTLE MOUNTAIN

A state historical marker in Mount Sterling makes no mention of Monk Estill, whose bravery in the Revolutionary War won his freedom from slavery.

"HERE ON MARCH 22, 1782, IN BATTLE OF LITTLE MOUNTAIN, CAPTAIN JAMES ESTILL AND 7 OF HIS FORCE OF 25 PIONEERS WERE KILLED IN DESPERATE HAND-TO-HAND FIGHTING WITH A BAND OF 25 MARAUDING WYANDOTS," the metal tablet on U.S. Highway 60 explains.

Among the survivors was Estill's servant, Monk, one of the most famous slaves in frontier Kentucky, according to *A History of Blacks in Kentucky: From Slavery to Segregation, 1760–1891* by Marion B. Lucas. Not only was Monk a hero at Little Mountain, but he had also played "a major role in preventing the destruction of Estill's Station," Lucas wrote.

Estill's Station was a small fort that Estill built fifteen miles south of Boonesborough in what is now Madison County. On March 20, 1782, Wyandot warriors had raided Estill's Station. The Indians tomahawked and scalped a teenage girl, seized Monk and evidently planned to wipe out the fort.

Had they tried, the Wyandots probably would have succeeded. Unknown to them, the upright log walls of Estill's Station sheltered only women, children and a man too ill to join Estill and his party.

Yet the quick-thinking Monk provided his captors with "a plausible but highly exaggerated account of the strength of the station and number of fighting men in it," according to *A History of Kentucky* by Lewis and Richard Collins. Monk's story was so convincing that the Indians left but with him still a captive.

As soon as Estill and the other men returned to the fort, they set out to avenge the attack. They trailed the Wyandots northeast through the wilderness, overtaking the Indians on March 22 in the vicinity of Little Mountain, the largest of about twenty-five prehistoric Indian mounds, for which Mount Sterling, the seat of Montgomery County, was named.

"During the battle," wrote Lucas, a Western Kentucky University historian and author, "the clever Monk shouted to his owner across the lines, giving the strength of the Indians and urging the frontiersmen on."

Estill, for whom Estill County was named, was first wounded by gunfire. A warrior finished the captain off by fatally stabbing him in a desperate fight the historians Collins likened to "two immense serpents struggling for the mastery."

Monk escaped from the Wyandots. But he claimed seventeen Indians perished in the skirmish, which lasted more than two hours. The fight was dubbed Estill's Defeat.

In the 1930s, the Daughters of the American Revolution erected a memorial closer to the actual battle site than the highway marker. The monument, which is on Owingsville Road, is an old millstone with a bronze plaque fastened to it. The plaque tells nothing of Monk's bravery in the battle. He is only named as "Negro 'Monk.'"

In his 1895 book, *The History of Kentucky*, Z.F. Smith wrote that Monk's heroism was "illustrative of the faithfulness and great bravery of the slaves, which were so often shown in times of peril to their masters and families." Lucas said Smith's characterization of Monk is typical of earlier white historians who claimed that "slavery was so 'mild' in the commonwealth that slaves felt no need to flee its bondage. These historians, especially during the frontier period of Kentucky history, cited as proof the fact that slaves and their owners often fought side-by-side against raiding Indians."

The French and Indian War and the American Revolution

Lucas said few slaves ran away to live with the Indians.

> *But their reluctance to flee bondage was not because Kentucky slavery was a "mild" form of servitude. When Indians attacked the homes of masters, they also attacked the cabins of slaves. Facing the hostile environment of wilderness and Indians, slaves understood that to run off into the forest might result in death. A safer, more secure life—but one of unrelieved labor—existed for them among their masters. And though they had no assurance, the future might offer a better opportunity for escape from the evil of slavery.*

After Estill's Defeat, Monk helped carry wounded frontiersmen to the safety of Estill's Station, Lucas wrote. In 1782, Estill's son, Wallace, freed Monk in gratitude for his bravery.

Monk Estill, who took his owner's surname, became a valuable citizen, Lucas wrote. He made gunpowder for Estill's Station and for Boonesborough, using saltpeter he found in a cave in Madison County.

"We Are All Slaughtered Now"

"The Martyrs of the Last Battle of the Revolution" are buried on an oak-shaded Kentucky hillside near where they fell in a bloody ambush that claimed the life of Daniel Boone's son.

A mass grave at Blue Licks State Resort Park near Mount Olivet, the Robertson County seat, holds the remains of forty-six Kentucky militia soldiers slain by Indians and white Loyalists on August 19, 1782. The Battle of Blue Licks went down in history as "the last battle of the American Revolution" and "one of the worst military disasters suffered by Americans on the Kentucky frontier," according to *The Kentucky Encyclopedia*.

The battle "was Kentucky's worst defeat" in the Revolutionary War, according to *A New History of Kentucky* by Lowell H. Harrison and James C. Klotter.

Blue Licks haunted Boone until his death thirty-eight years later. "Whenever Boone spoke of the…defeat he was overcome with grief and wept openly," Faragher wrote in *Daniel Boone*.

A rough-hewn boulder memorializes the grave site at one-hundred-acre Blue Licks Park in northeastern Kentucky. "The Martyrs of the Last Battle of the Revolution Lie Buried Here" reads their epitaph on a bronze plaque bolted to the rock.

Licking River, where Boone and the militia crossed. *Courtesy of the author.*

Blue Licks battlefield marker. *Courtesy of the author.*

The French and Indian War and the American Revolution

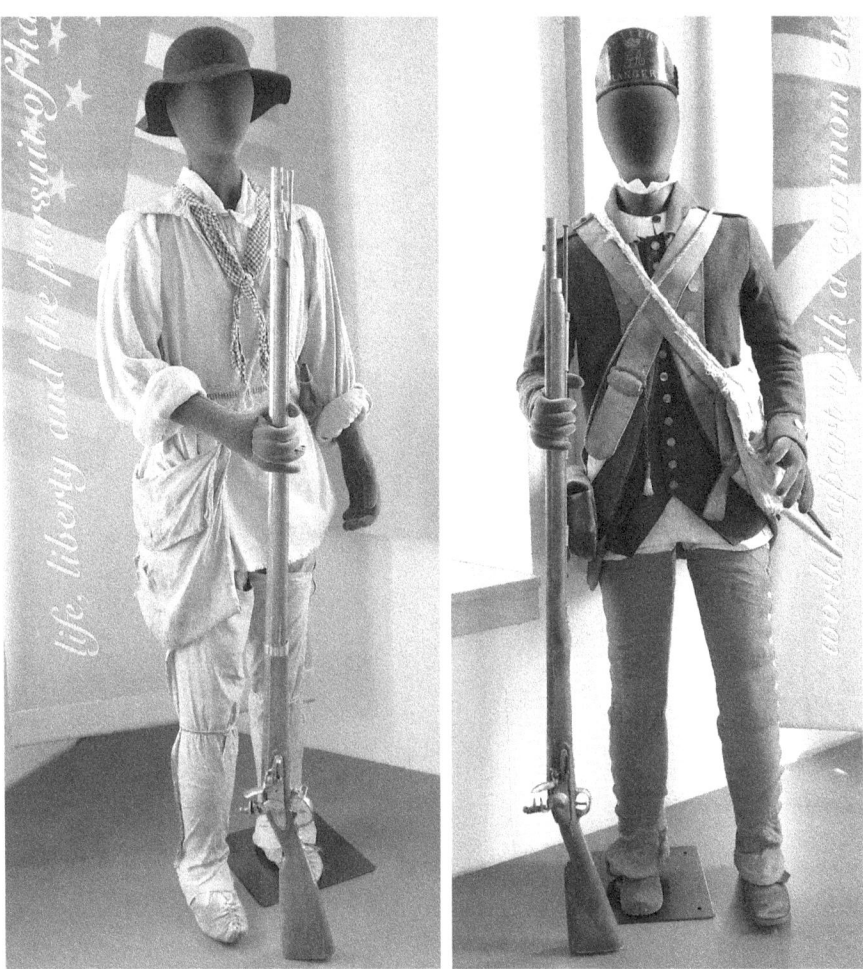

Above left: Mannequin dressed as a militia soldier in the Blue Licks State Resort Park museum. *Courtesy of by the author.*

Above right: Mannequin dressed as a Loyalist soldier in the Blue Licks State Resort Park museum. *Courtesy of the author.*

Israel Boone's remains are not among them. "Daniel was able to recover the body and brought him back to Boone's Station [now a state historic site not far from Lexington] where he was laid to rest," said Paul Tierney, park naturalist.

The names of "the heroic pioneers" who "fought and fell," defending Kentucky, are carved on a stone shaft near the mass grave. As many as eighty Kentuckians were killed in the battle, according to Tierney.

Mannequin dressed as Native American warrior in the Blue Licks State Resort Park museum. *Courtesy of the author.*

The thirty-one-foot marble obelisk, erected by the State of Kentucky in 1928, also recognized the victors, naming the Native American tribes they represented: Ottawa, Chippewa, Shawnee, Delaware, Wyandot and Mingo. "Paying tribute to Native Americans was unheard of at the time," Tierney said.

The raider leader, American-born Captain William Caldwell, is quoted on the stone: "They [the Kentuckians] advanced in the divisions in good order and gave us a volley and stood to it very well for some time."

Boone's words are carved on another side of the memorial: "So valiantly did our small party fight, that, to the memory of those who unfortunately fell in the battle, enough of honor cannot be paid."

The battle pitted 182 Kentuckians against a force of about 300 Indians and 50 whites, according to Harrison and Klotter. The whites were from Butler's Rangers, a pro-British guerrilla group mostly from New York state. The enemy also included the most hated American Loyalist, Simon Girty—"Dirty Girty" to Kentuckians.

The raiders struck Bryan's Station, near Lexington, on August 15. After pinning the settlers in their fort for two days, they withdrew, "killing cattle, burning buildings, and damaging crops outside the station," Harrison and Klotter wrote.

The French and Indian War and the American Revolution

Right: Blue Licks battlefield monument. *Courtesy of the author.*

Below: William Shannon's grave marker. *Courtesy of the author.*

Monument "to honor those individuals whose names were omitted from the original monument." *Courtesy of the author.*

On August 18, militiamen from several settlements rendezvoused at Bryan's Station. The volunteers included the Boones.

Reinforcements were on the way. But Colonel John Todd, the militia commander, decided not to wait.

The Native Americans and rangers were on foot. The Kentuckians gave chase on horseback.

Boone suspected a trap. "The retreating Indians and rangers made no effort to conceal their tracks," Harrison and Klotter wrote.

On August 19, the militia caught up with the raiders at the Lower Blue Licks crossing of the Licking River, about thirty-eight miles north of Bryan's Station. Boone believed the foe was hiding on the other side.

He suggested they split up and attack on foot, hitting the raiders in a pincer movement. Major Hugh McGary called Boone a coward for not wanting to attack head on.

McGary waded into the shallow stream with a challenge sure to stir the Kentuckians. Anybody who didn't follow him across the Licking was yellow, he yelled.

"A rush ensued, and even cautious men saw no choice but to join in the crossing," Harrison and Klotter wrote. "'Come on,' Boone said to his militiamen, 'we are all slaughtered now.'"

The French and Indian War and the American Revolution

They scrambled up the hillside where the rangers and their Native American allies were concealed in wooded ravines, according to Tierney. The enemy raked the Kentuckians with deadly musket fire. Fierce hand-to-hand fighting followed.

The battle became a rout as the militia soldiers fled to their horses on the other side of the river. The Indians were close behind.

Some men escaped on horseback, others on foot. McGary was among the survivors. Todd, whose brother was Mary Todd Lincoln's grandfather, was killed and, apparently, buried in the mass grave. Todd County is named for him.

The Indians stopped pursuing the militia "after a mile or two," Harrison and Klotter wrote. They returned to the battlefield "to plunder…and scalp and mutilate the bodies of the dead Kentuckians," the authors added.

The Battle of Blue Licks hardly could have been more one-sided. Harrison and Klotter put ranger-Indian losses at "about ten men killed and fourteen wounded." Caldwell reported his only losses were three Indians killed, according to Tierney.

Within a day or two of the battle, Boone was back at Bryan's Station helping organize a burial party for his dead comrades "who still lay on the ground at the Blue Licks," Faragher wrote. They approached the Licking on August 24, long rifles at the ready and prepared to avenge the defeat of Todd and his men should the rangers, Native Americans and Girty still be on the battlefield.

They were gone. But the Kentuckians spied "flocks of vultures" circling in the summer sky and witnessed "the horrible spectacle of the birds gorging themselves on the bodies that lay black and bloated after five days in the August heat," Faragher wrote.

The author said most of the dead men "had been scalped, and their bodies were so mangled and distended that it was difficult to identify them positively." Boone found the body of his son, who had been shot to death. Israel Boone had been scalped, his clothes torn away and his corpse "partly devoured by wild beasts," wrote Peter Houston in *A Sketch of the Life and Character of Daniel Boone*. He said the other bodies were "in like condition."

Apparently, some of the Kentuckians were killed after they were captured, either on the battlefield or at Indian settlements north of the nearby Ohio River. "Some of the slashed disfigured corpses [at Blue Licks] still had their hands tied," Lofaro wrote in *The Life and Adventures of Daniel Boone*.

Evidently, many remains were not recovered. Lofaro explained that Boone and the others "buried the bodies they could find in a common grave." Houston said forty-six corpses were interred.

Tierney said a "crude limestone slab" marked the burial pit for many years.

Seven years after the obelisk was unveiled, the Daughters of the American Revolution placed the current gravestone. Next to it is a small, flat bronze marker to William Shannon, one of the "martyrs."

In 1999, descendants of John Childress—who survived Blue Licks—and the Kentucky Department of Parks added a smaller stone, near the old obelisk, "to honor those individuals whose names were omitted from the original monument." Its inscription reads:

THOMAS BOONE
KILLED
JOHN CHILDRESS
ESCAPED
JAMES LEDGERWOOD
CAPTURED BUT ESCAPED
JAMES WARD
ESCAPED

"We still don't know exactly how many Kentuckians were killed at Blue Licks," Tierney said. "But it was likely between seventy-eight and eighty."

CHAPTER 2

THE WAR OF 1812

"THE MILITIA PIG"

Apparently nobody knows where Governor Isaac Shelby, a War of 1812 veteran and Kentucky's first chief executive, might have buried his adopted Militia Pig. "I don't think the pig is in the Shelby family cemetery," said Brenda Willoughby, retired manager at Constitution Square State Historic Site in Danville. "But I would assume if it was a pet, it would have been buried somewhere."

Willoughby also oversaw the Isaac Shelby Cemetery State Historic Site. That property is in Lincoln County, five miles south of Danville, seat of Boyle County. The plot contains the graves of Shelby, his wife and others.

A sign at the site is silent about the sow. The porker purportedly retired "in ease and indolence" on Shelby's farm, according to Lewis Collins's *Historical Sketches of Kentucky*.

In 1813, the Militia Pig joined Harrodsburg-area recruits heading to Canada to battle the British. The men hadn't gone far when they spied "two pigs fighting, and delayed their march to see it out," Collins wrote. The winner fell in with the troops, waddling all the way to the Ohio River, opposite Cincinnati, where the soldiers caught a ferryboat. The sow swam the river and waited "on the other side until the whole cortege crossed over," Collins wrote.

The volunteers eventually rendezvoused with Shelby, a Revolutionary War hero who was elected governor in 1792, when Kentucky became a

Governor Isaac Shelby. *Courtesy of the Kentucky Historical Society.*

state, and won another term in 1812. He got special permission from the General Assembly to lead Bluegrass State soldiers in the War of 1812.

"On the whole journey, as the men grew more familiar with their comrade, it became a pet, receiving a full share of the rations issued to the soldiers, and destitute as the troops found themselves at times of sustenance, no one thought of putting the knife to the throat of their fellow soldier," Collins wrote.

When the troops reached Lake Erie, the ham on the lam refused to go to Canada. Some of the Kentuckians attributed her behavior not to cowardice but to "constitutional scruples," the historian explained. Collins claimed the hog knew no "militia pig" could be forced to fight on foreign soil against his—or her—will.

The American army failed to conquer Canada and ultimately returned stateside. When the Kentucky troops re-crossed Lake Erie, they found the pig "ready to resume her march with the rest," Collins wrote.

It was winter, which made the trek to Kentucky doubly difficult for the dispirited soldiers. They were cold, tired and hungry. Even so, nobody turned the sow into pork chops.

The War of 1812

The Militia Pig "suffered greatly on its homeward march" and finally collapsed at Maysville, Collins wrote. Shelby left the pig "in trusty hands" to recuperate and then sent for the swine, which apparently spent the rest of her days in an earthly hog heaven.

Traveller's Rest, Shelby's brick home, burned long ago. A 1900s-vintage house stands on the spot. Tombstones mark the graves of Shelby and other beloved family members. If the Militia Pig was buried and had a monument, it is gone.

"Rumpsey Dumpsey"

It might not swing many votes in a modern political campaign, but "Rumpsey dumpsey, rumpsey dumpsey, Colonel Johnson killed Tecumseh" was Richard Mentor Johnson's slogan when he ran for vice president in 1836.

The Kentucky Democrat was elected in 1837 by the U.S. Senate because "no candidate received a majority of the electoral votes," according to the *Kentucky Encyclopedia*. Never before—or since—had a vice president been so chosen.

Johnson was from Great Crossing, near Georgetown, the Scott County seat. He never claimed he ended the life of Tecumseh, the famous Shawnee chief, in the War of 1812. But he didn't stop anybody from saying he did.

Tecumseh fell in the 1813 Battle of the Thames in Canada. Who killed him is unknown. "Johnson may have been the one," Klotter said. "Others were said to have shot Tecumseh. So it is still a mystery."

Johnson's own recollections of the battle, an American victory, do not solve the riddle either. The colonel, who left his seat in Congress to command a regiment of Kentucky mounted riflemen, said only that he shot "an Indian chief."

Even so, he was dubbed "the Hero of the Thames," a bloody clash he barely survived. The colonel was "covered with wounds, twenty-five balls having been shot into him, his clothes, and his horse," according to *A History of Kentucky*. Johnson's bravery had "scarcely a parallel in the heroic annals of our country," the authors added.

Fought near Fairfield, Ontario, on October 5, 1813, the Battle of the Thames pitted about 3,000 American troops against a force of around 4,500 British soldiers and their Native American allies, according to *A New History of Kentucky*.

"Johnson's Kentucky Mounted Rifles, divided in two sections, rode through the British regulars and routed them in a matter of minutes," Harrison and

Johnson monument. *Courtesy of the author.*

Klotter wrote. "When the half regiment led by Johnson encountered heavy fire from Indians who were concealed in the heavy growth of a swamp, Johnson dismounted his men to fight on foot."

Still astride his horse, Johnson summoned a twenty-man "Forlorn Hope" to draw the Indians' fire. "Fifteen were killed at once, and four were wounded," Harrison and Klotter wrote. Among the slain was sixty-four-year-old Lincoln County pioneer William Whitley.

Meanwhile, Johnson, according to the Collins book,

> *was in the very midst and thickest of the fight, inspiring by his presence and courage the utmost confidence of his brave followers, and though perforated with balls, his bridle arm shattered, and bleeding profusely, he continued to fight until he encountered and slew an Indian chief who formed the rallying point of the savages. This chief was supposed to be the famous Tecumseh himself, upon whose fall the Indians raised a yell and retreated.*

The War of 1812

Johnson monument bas-relief. *Courtesy of the author.*

Johnson made political hay off the Battle of the Thames, especially the claim that he killed Tecumseh. In 1814, he went back to the House as a war hero.

In 1819, he was elected to the state House of Representatives. That year, Johnson was named to serve out the U.S. Senate term of John J. Crittenden, who had resigned. The legislature reelected him to the Senate, where he served until 1837, according to the *Kentucky Encyclopedia*.

Johnson was a strong supporter of President Andrew Jackson, who chose Vice President Martin Van Buren to succeed him in 1836. Old Hickory also persuaded the Democratic National Convention to nominate his Senate ally, Johnson, for vice president.

Not everybody approved of Kentucky's "Hero of the Thames." Some southern delegates hated Johnson for "openly living with his slave mistress and raising their two daughters pretty much as his own," Klotter said. According to Paul F. Boller Jr.'s book, *Presidential Campaigns*, Virginia's delegation stormed out of the hall over Johnson's nomination, hissing "most ungraciously."

Nonetheless, most Democrats supported their party's ticket against a trio of Whigs, including General William Henry Harrison, who led American forces at the Battle of the Thames. But Boller added that the Whigs wondered if "a lucky shot, even if it did hit Tecumseh, qualifies a man for vice president."

Harrison ousted Van Buren for the presidency in 1840, and Johnson came home to Scott County. He served two more terms in the state House of Representatives, died in office in 1850 at age sixty-nine and was buried in the Frankfort Cemetery. A bas-relief carved on the base of the tall column that marks Johnson's last resting place shows him shooting an Indian chief, though old Rumpsey Dumpsey's head is broken off.

"His career as a legislator, was scarcely less brilliant and useful, than that in which he distinguished himself as a warrior," Collins wrote. In 1843, the General Assembly created Johnson County in his honor.

The Sportsman's Hill Scalp

Did William Whitley ask his fellow Kentuckians to scalp him if he fell to the foe?

Supposedly, Whitley, who was killed at the Battle of the Thames, told his comrades in arms to lift his hair should British soldiers or Indian warriors slay him. "He knew his body couldn't be brought home for burial," Patty Pope said. "He thought his scalp could be. But that may be just folklore."

Pope was a part-time guide at the William Whitley House State Historic Site near Stanford, the Lincoln County seat. The two-story dwelling was Kentucky's first brick house, according to Pope.

There is no record of Whitley's scalp being interred at Sportsman's Hill, the Whitley estate. "But it's a story that has been told for a long time," Pope said.

Born in Virginia, Whitley moved to Kentucky in 1775. He fought Indians during the American Revolution, and after Kentucky became a state, he served a term in the legislature.

Whitley was fiercely anti-British. When he built a racetrack near his house, he had horses run counterclockwise on clay, rather than clockwise on grass, as in Britain. "To this day, all American sports using oval tracks race counterclockwise," *The Kentucky Encyclopedia* advises.

Whitley was able to soldier in his sixties because he "was a man above the ordinary size, of great muscular power, and capable of enduring great fatigue and privation," according to *A History of Kentucky*.

Whitley reportedly was buried where he fell at the Thames battle. The grave is unmarked.

Part of the battlefield is preserved in a small roadside park that features a stone memorial to Tecumseh, who perished in the battle.

Whitley was also credited with shooting Tecumseh. "According to other legends, Whitley killed Tecumseh or Tecumseh killed Whitley," Pope said. "We don't have any proof of that either."

In any event, Whitley was not forgotten. "Whitley County, Kentucky, and Whitley County, Indiana, are named for him," Pope said.

"Burgoyne Cannon" Was Thames Battle Trophy

A little cannon is a big attraction at the Kentucky Military History Museum in Frankfort.

The brass-barreled, British-made howitzer changed hands three times in two conflicts, according to James Russell Harris, senior associate editor of *The Register*, the Kentucky Historical Society's scholarly journal. Kentucky soldiers grabbed the gun for good in the Battle of the Thames.

"Most of the troops in the Battle of the Thames were Kentuckians," Harris said. "They considered the victory theirs."

An American army first captured the cannon in the Revolutionary War. The gun belonged to General John Burgoyne's redcoat forces at the Battle of Saratoga in 1777.

The Americans, led by General Horatio Gates, grabbed more than the gun. They bagged Burgoyne and his whole army. "That's why the cannon is called the 'Burgoyne Cannon,'" Harris explained.

The British reclaimed the cannon when they seized Fort Detroit in June 1812. "Rumpsy Dumpsey" Johnson and his Kentucky Mounted Rifles were credited with retaking the cannon at the Battle of the Thames.

Governor Shelby, who was chief of Bluegrass State troops in the battle, brought the cannon back to Frankfort as a war trophy. He apparently had it displayed in the state capitol.

The vintage weapon has been in the military history museum since the facility opened under the auspices of the historical society in the Old State Arsenal in 1974, according to Harris. "It is one of the most prized artifacts," he said.

The shiny barrel still bears its original British markings. The cannon's gray-painted, wheeled wooden carriage is a reproduction, Harris said.

The gun, which shot three-pound cannonballs, is guarded by a pair of musket-toting mannequins. They are dressed in fringed black and red hunting shirts and plumed top hats, the distinctive uniform of Johnson's hard-fighting horsemen.

"Some Great Spirit of Death"

Friend and foe alike remembered Ephraim Brank's marksmanship in the Battle of New Orleans.

The Muhlenberg County militia soldier was a hero to the victorious Americans. He was "some great spirit of death" to the vanquished British.

"We lost the battle," a redcoat officer lamented, "and to my mind, the Kentucky rifleman contributed more to our defeat than anything else."

Brank's Bluegrass State comrades in arms told and retold the story of him alone atop the battlements, gunning down enemy soldiers as calmly as he bagged squirrels back home. "All during the battle, soldiers kept loading and reloading rifles and handing them up to him," said Roberta Chumley, a county historian. "Ephraim Brank kept shooting and he never missed."

A lawyer, land surveyor and farmer, Brank was not forgotten in Greenville, the Muhlenberg County seat. There is a Brank Street. The old soldier is buried in an honored spot in the town cemetery; a military tombstone marks his grave.

Brank's tombstone. *Courtesy of the author.*

The War of 1812

Cannon and reconstructed American battle line. *Courtesy of the author.*

"There's even a 'Ballad of Ephraim Brank,'" Chumley said. "Historically, he's our most famous citizen."

Born in North Carolina in 1791, Brank settled in Muhlenberg County about 1808. "Captain Brank was a man of stately proportions and wonderful physical constitution," Otto A. Rothert wrote in *History of Muhlenberg County*. "He was a 'crack shot' and an enthusiastic hunter: a well-read and a resolute and systematic man, and very kind to those with whom he came in contact."

Except redcoats, Chumley added. "The way I've always heard the story is that General Andrew Jackson, the commander at New Orleans, told the Kentuckians to 'Get on down to New Orleans as fast as you can even if you don't have enough rifles,'" she said.

Some Kentuckians did arrive unarmed, astonishing Jackson. "I have never seen a Kentuckian without a gun and a pack of cards and a bottle of whiskey in my life," Old Hickory declared, according to Harrison and Klotter's book.

Chumley isn't sure if Brank mowed down the British with his trusty squirrel rifle.

Anyway, Jackson deployed his little army behind strong earthworks south of the city and awaited the British attack, which came on January 8, 1815. The battlefield, which includes cannons and reconstructed American earthworks, is just down the Mississippi River from New Orleans. The site is part of the Jean Lafitte National Historical Park and Preserve.

New Orleans turned out to be the bloodiest battle of the War of 1812, which, unknown to either army, had been ended by a peace treaty signed at Ghent, Belgium, on December 24, 1814.

The British charged; the Americans, whom the redcoats scorned as "dirty shirts," held their ground. They poured a deadly rain of rifle, musket and cannon fire into the attackers, forcing them to retreat.

The Americans suffered fewer than twenty casualties. More than two thousand British troops perished, including their commander, General Sir Edward Packenham. How many enemy soldiers Brank shot to death is not known.

But the British officer whose account of the battle Rothert included in his book said Brank was plainly visible, standing solo on the breastworks, where "he seemed to grow, phantom-like, higher and higher, assuming, through the smoke, the supernatural appearance of some great spirit of death." The redcoat added, "Again, did he reload and discharge, and reload and discharge his rifle, with the same unfailing aim and the same unfailing result."

As the British neared the American line, which was fronted by a ditch, they were shrouded by thick battle smoke. It was, the officer remembered, a time of "indescribable pleasure" because it hid them and shut "that spectral hunter from our gaze."

The officer described Brank as "a tall man standing on the breastworks, dressed in linsey-woolsey, with buckskin leggings, and a broad-brimmed felt hat that fell round the face, almost concealing the features. He was standing in one of those picturesque, graceful attitudes peculiar to those natural men dwelling in the forests."

Actually, Brank lived in a comfortable house in Greenville, where he returned after the war. Twice married and the father of five children, he died in 1885. "Ephraim McLean Brank's heroic act on the breastworks in the battle of New Orleans…is one of the most thrilling incidents recorded of any Muhlenberg man, as it is a fine one in our national history," Rothert wrote.

The War of 1812

"He Was Always Ready to Take Advantage of an Opportunity"

General James H. Wilkinson doesn't fit the town founder mold.

The man who platted Frankfort was a schemer, if not twice a traitor. "He was the sort of person who would make Benedict Arnold seem like a patriot," Harrison said.

Nonetheless, Wilkinson Street in Kentucky's capital is named for the Maryland-born general whose incompetence in the War of 1812 ended his checkered military career. Wilkinson was one of the most unsavory characters in Bluegrass State history, according to Harrison.

Allegedly, Wilkinson plotted to pry Kentucky from the United States in 1787 and 1804. His coconspirators supposedly were Spain and the infamous Aaron Burr. "James Wilkinson lived a life of intrigue," according to *A New History of Kentucky*. "No superior was safe from his machinations."

During the American Revolution, Wilkinson served under Generals Horatio Gates and George Washington. But Washington mistrusted him as a conniver and for good reason. Wilkinson was part of the notorious Conway Cabal, a group of officers who tried to depose Washington and possibly replace him with Gates.

After the war, Wilkinson settled in Kentucky, speculated in land and landed in debt. He looked to Spain to bail him out. In 1787, he told the governor of Spanish New Orleans that Kentucky was close to separating from Virginia, its parent state.

Wilkinson suggested he could deliver Kentucky to Spain if the price was right. "He wanted a trade monopoly, a royal pension, and a suitable rank and position if Kentucky became associated with Spain," Harrison and Klotter wrote.

The governor gave Wilkinson permission to sell up to $37,000 worth of produce in the Crescent City, after which the general headed home. He sailed to the East Coast and then traveled to Kentucky aboard "a four-wheeled carriage pulled by a perfectly matched team and with black servants as outriders," according to the Harrison and Klotter book.

It is not known if Wilkinson really planned to deal Kentucky to Spain or just wanted to fatten his wallet at the expense of a gullible governor. The episode went down in history as the Spanish Conspiracy.

Meanwhile, Wilkinson laid out Frankfort, which the Virginia legislature incorporated in 1791, according to *The Kentucky Encyclopedia*. The state legislature named Frankfort the state capital in 1792.

Two years later, Wilkinson seemed to redeem his reputation by fighting bravely in the Battle of the Fallen Timbers. An American victory, the fight greatly reduced Indian power in the future state of Ohio.

In 1805, President Thomas Jefferson named Wilkinson governor of the new Louisiana territory. He was soon in hot water again.

After the general's old friend, Vice President Aaron Burr, shot Alexander Hamilton in a famous duel, the discredited and disgruntled Burr supposedly planned to carve a new nation from U.S. territory west of the Appalachian Mountains, including Kentucky, and make himself emperor.

Allegedly, Wilkinson was part of the so-called Burr Conspiracy. In 1805, he and Burr met secretly at Fort Massac on the Ohio River in southern Illinois. (The site, which is in the town of Metropolis, is a state park that includes a reconstructed fort.) What plot, if any, Burr and Wilkinson hatched at the tiny frontier outpost is still a mystery.

In any event, Wilkinson was accused of abusing his power as Louisiana's governor and was removed. At the same time, the general got cold feet and turned on Burr.

Wilkinson sent a self-serving letter to Jefferson, purportedly proving Burr was a traitor. Wilkinson's "evidence" was bogus; Burr was tried for treason and acquitted in 1807. Wilkinson was court-martialed five years later but found innocent.

He was back on active duty in time for the War of 1812. But he proved an inept commander, losing the Battles of Crysler's Farm in 1813 and Lacolle Mill, both in Canada. Afterward, President Madison relieved him.

Wilkinson ended up in Mexico City, where he died in 1825 at age sixty-eight. Harrison said it is impossible to know if Frankfort's founder was a two-time traitor or was just plain greedy. "I think he played things by ear," the historian suggested. "He was always ready to take advantage of an opportunity."

CHAPTER 3

THE TEXAS REVOLUTION AND THE MEXICAN-AMERICAN WAR

"THEIR BODIES WERE LEFT UNBURIED ON THE PRAIRIE"

Nineteen martyrs of the Texas Revolution are all but unknown in their hometown.

Mexican troops captured and executed Captain Amon B. King and his eighteen Paducah Volunteers after the 1836 Battle of Refugio, Texas. "Their bodies were left unburied on the prairie," says the *Handbook of Texas Online*. Refugio citizens gathered the remains and buried them in a cemetery near their town, which began as a Spanish mission on the Mission River.

King was the Paducah marshal when he and his little band left to fight in Texas. They departed on a steamboat with Captain Peyton S. Wyatt's company of volunteers from Huntsville, Alabama, the *Handbook* says.

The Alabamians spent a day and two nights in Paducah, James M. Robertson wrote in the *Southwestern Historical Quarterly* in 1925. (He described them as Georgians.)

In any event, Wyatt's volunteers "marched upon the streets of Paducah with their band of music making talks and appeals throughout the City as they went, telling of their mission to Texas and urging young men to join them on their mission," Robertson explained.

Wyatt and his men won over King, who

> *resigned his office as City Marshal, [and] bade his sweetheart a final good-bye, assuring her that immediately at the close of the Texas Revolution he would return for her and they would be married...Among the effects of Amon B. King of that time was a large wooly dog to which he was greatly attached, and he left his dog in the care of his expected wife, and joined the Wyatt Company.*

At some point, King, who was the city marshal in 1833, decided to organize his own company from the dozen and a half Paducah men who agreed to go to Texas with him. They became the Paducah Volunteers, with King as their captain, the *Handbook* says.

The King and Wyatt companies traveled together down the Ohio and Mississippi Rivers to Natchez, Mississippi. The men crossed the Mississippi into Louisiana and journeyed the rest of the way overland. On Christmas Day, they reported to General Sam Houston, commander of the Texas army, at Washington-on-the-Brazos, according to Robertson and the *Handbook*.

The next day, Texas, home to more than thirty thousand American immigrants, declared its independence from Mexico. Almost all of the rebels were American southerners; many of them brought their slaves. The southerners hoped Texas would become a U.S. slave state, especially after Mexico abolished slavery.

Mexico's ruler, General Antonio Lopez de Santa Anna, led about 6,000 soldiers into Texas to crush the revolt. He went down in Texas history as the Lone Star State's worst villain because he wiped out all 250 defenders of the Alamo, the famous fortified mission in San Antonio, in a thirteen-day siege that ended on March 6, 1836.

By then, almost all of the American settlers had fled Refugio. A few families remained and appealed to Colonel James Fannin for help against Mexicans and Indians, who they claimed were plundering abandoned homes, the *Handbook* says.

On March 10, Fannin sent King and twenty-eight men to help evacuate the families and bring back supplies. He arrived the next day and discovered that most of the settlers had taken refuge in the mission. But others, including the family of Lewis T. Ayers, were nearby at Esteban Lopez's ranch, according to the *Handbook*.

On March 12, King and his men went to the ranch and retrieved Ayers's wife, Rebecca. In addition, King's band arrested some Mexicans, who told

The Texas Revolution and the Mexican-American War

them that the reputed Mexican and Indian marauders were camped on a ranch eight miles distant, the *Handbook* says.

King had orders to immediately return to Goliad with the settlers. But he took about sixteen men—including Lewis T. Ayers, Fannin's newly appointed assistant quartermaster—and went after the Mexicans and Indians accused of pillaging Refugio. On the way, a group of Mexican ranchers and, reportedly, some Indians ambushed King's force, according to the *Handbook*.

King and his party fought their way back to Refugio on March 12 and took cover in the mission. Even so, they were not out of danger; Mexican ranchers surrounded Refugio. "Many Mexican rancheros from the San Patricio, Refugio, and Goliad areas had been incensed at their treatment by the Americans in Fannin's command and therefore remained loyal to Mexico and served as independent scouts and advance units for [the Mexican army of General Jose] Urrea," the *Handbook* explains.

King had only twenty-six men; six were separated during the retreat to Refugio. Some of Urrea's troops arrived at Refugio to increase the Mexican force to about two hundred men, according to the *Handbook*.

King managed to get word to Fannin that he needed help. On March 13, Lieutenant Colonel William Ward arrived with the Georgia Battalion and part of Wyatt's company. The forces of King, Ward and Wyatt broke the siege. Now, the escape route to Goliad was open. But King refused to go until he had gotten even with some of the rancheros, at least, the *Handbook* says.

"His insubordination was one of a number of events that led to Fannin's ultimate disaster, the Goliad Massacre," according to the *Handbook*.

> *Apparently, both Ward's and King's men were eager to fight the Mexicans, but a disagreement erupted between the two commanders about who should carry out the mission; King wanted the task, but Ward preferred his second in command, Warren J. Mitchell. Taking his own company and eighteen of Wyatt's men, King sallied forth on his own punitive expedition…while Ward sent Mitchell to reconnoiter the enemy and waited at the mission for their return.*

Meanwhile, Urrea approached Refugio with his main body of troops, about 1,500 men. Seeing the Mexicans, Mitchell returned to the mission, and Urrea attacked, the *Handbook* says.

On March 14, after ambushing and killing eight Mexicans as they sat around a campfire, King headed back to Refugio. But Urrea's troops blocked the way, prompting a skirmish. "King and his party put up a brave fight that lasted from late morning until dark," the *Handbook* explains. "King's arm was shattered by a musketball; one of his men was killed and four were wounded. Mexican casualties were apparently heavier; but sources are unreliable."

During the night, King and his men crossed the river, hoping to escape to Goliad. But their powder got wet, rendering them defenseless. The Mexicans captured King and his band on March 15, bound them and took them back to Refugio, from which Ward and most of his troops had managed to escape, according to the *Handbook*.

Urrea ordered King and thirty-two other prisoners marched out of town and shot. En route to the execution site, a German mercenary serving as an officer in the Mexican army heard some of the condemned men speaking his native tongue, according to the *Handbook*. (Some Germans had settled in Texas.)

The officer ordered the firing squad and the prisoners back to Refugio, where he released the two German speakers and six Refugio settlers, including Ayers, the *Handbook* says. But for King and the remaining twenty-four prisoners, it was only a twenty-four-hour stay of execution. They were marched back out to their deaths the next day. The Mexicans forced the men "to walk through prickly pears with their bare feet" and shot them, Robertson wrote.

Ward survived only eleven more days. He and what was left of his command were among four hundred Texan prisoners, including Fannin, shot by the Mexicans at Goliad on March 27, seven days after their victory over the Texans at the nearby Battle of Coleto Creek.

"Remember the Alamo!" and "Remember Goliad!" were war cries in the Texas Revolution. Texas won its independence in 1836, becoming the Republic of Texas. It was admitted to the Union as a slave state in 1845.

The Alamo became a shrine. A monument marks the mass grave of the Goliad martyrs.

The final resting place of King and his men "was forgotten until May 9, 1934, when a grave containing sixteen skeletons was discovered by accident in Mount Calvary Catholic Cemetery near Refugio," the *Handbook* says. "The bones were identified as those of King's men and on June 17, 1934, they were reinterred in the cemetery with appropriate religious and military ceremonies."

In honor of the Texas centennial celebration of 1936, the state erected memorials to King and his men in Refugio and in the cemetery. "Tradition has it that another grave in the vicinity of the cemetery contains the bones of other victims," according to the *Handbook*.

"Though the battle of Refugio is one of the less-known engagements of the Texas Revolution, its consequences are significant," the *Handbook* says.

The Texas Revolution and the Mexican-American War

Fannin disastrously split his forces by ordering King and Ward into the path of Urrea's army, a move that reduced by about 150 the number of men he was able to bring to bear against the Mexicans at the battle of Coleto [on March 19–20, which Fannin lost].

King and Ward, whose quarrel over rank divided their own small force, refused to return to Goliad before engaging Mexican troops. This prevented their rejoining Fannin, thereby delaying Fannin's retreat to Victoria—a delay that contributed to his defeat at the Coleto and resulted as well in the Texas misfortune in the battle of Refugio and the execution of King's men. Most historians have judged the entire episode as folly. The clash of stubborn personalities, together with their contempt for the prowess of the Mexican army, reduced Fannin's, Ward's, and King's effectiveness, contributing to their defeat and to the calamity of the Goliad Massacre.

"The Most Gifted of All His children and His Favorite"

Almost six hundred Kentuckians died in the Mexican-American War, including the son and namesake of Henry Clay, who opposed the conflict.

"This is no war of defense, but one of unnecessary and offensive aggression," Clay protested.

Henry Clay Jr. fell at the Battle of Buena Vista in 1847. "My life has been full of domestic afflictions, but this is the last and the severest," Carl Schurz quoted Clay's lamentation. In his book, *Life of Henry Clay: American Statesman*, Schurz also wrote that Henry Jr. "was the most gifted of all his children and his favorite."

While his father warned against the war, Clay recruited the Second Regiment of Foot, Kentucky Volunteers. He became its lieutenant colonel.

Born in 1811, Clay graduated from Transylvania University at age seventeen and West Point at age twenty. He returned to Lexington and became a lawyer, like his famous father. He also joined the Whig Party of Clay Sr. and served in the Kentucky House of Representatives from 1835 to 1837.

Despite Clay's criticism of the war, most Kentuckians embraced the conflict. More than five thousand Kentuckians signed up to fight, according to the *Kentucky Encyclopedia*.

Clay was conciliatory toward the volunteers, according to Robert Remini's book, *Henry Clay: Statesman for the Union*. The historian quoted Clay: "We cannot but admire and approve the patriotic and gallant spirit which

Grave of Henry Clay Jr., Frankfort Cemetery. *Courtesy of the author.*

animates our Country men, altho' we might wish that the cause in which they have stept forth was more reconcilable with the dictates of conscience." Remini also wrote that, when Clay Jr. left for war, "father and son embraced in a tearful farewell." Clay Sr., according to Remini, presented "young Henry with a pair of pistols to carry with him in battle."

Clay Jr.'s regiment was in the thick of battle at Buena Vista on February 23. The Americans, under General Zachary Taylor, who had lived in Louisville, defeated the Mexicans under Santa Anna.

Buena Vista was Taylor's greatest victory. Although Clay and many other Whigs had denounced the war, Taylor, its greatest hero, would run for president as a Whig in 1848 and win. Clay would be his chief rival for the Whig nomination.

But 260 of Taylor's troops died at Buena Vista, including Clay and Colonel Robert McKee, the Second Foot's commander. They perished with dozens more Americans in a dusty, sun-baked gorge.

The Texas Revolution and the Mexican-American War

"It would be a sad task indeed to name over all who fell during this… slaughter," wrote Captain James Henry Carelton of the First Dragoons in *The Battle of Buena Vista with the Operations of the "Army of Occupation" for One Month*, a book published in 1848. "The whole gorge, from the plateau to the mouth, was strewn with our dead; *all* dead; no wounded there, not a man; for the infantry had rushed down the sides, and completed the work with the bayonet."

Clay learned of Henry Jr.'s death from another son, James B. Clay, according to Remini. The family was eating dinner at Ashland, Clay's Lexington mansion, when James "entered the room 'with grief depicted in his countenance.'"

Lieutenant Colonel Clay had been shot in the thigh. "He ordered his men to withdraw, surrendering to one of them the pistols his father had given him," Remini wrote. "'Leave me, take care of yourselves,' he said. 'Take these Pistols to my father, and tell him, that I have done all I can with them, and now return them to him.'"

As the Mexican troops approached, Clay tried to defend himself with his sword. But he was bayoneted to death, according to Remini.

Taylor wrote Clay, expressing his "deepest and most heartfelt sympathies for your irreparable loss." He added that, under young Clay's leadership, "the sons of Kentucky, in the thickest of the strife, upheld the honor of the State and of the country." Remini wrote that a brother officer sent Clay a lock of his son's hair, taken from his head after the body was recovered. Clay wore it in a "breast pin" and willed it to his grandson, Henry Clay III, according to the author.

Henry Jr.'s death shattered his father. Remini wrote:

> *His favorite son, his namesake, on whom he had pinned his greatest hopes and who even resembled him, had given his life "for this most unnecessary and horrible war with Mexico." Tears streamed down his face as the full realization of what had happened sunk in. Devastated, he bowed his head, covered his face with his hands, and gave full vent to his grief.*

The remains of Clay and several other Kentuckians killed in the Mexican-American War were returned to Kentucky for burial in the Frankfort Cemetery. Clay was interred on July 20, 1847, according to Remini.

"Stop Your Nonsense and Drink Your Whiskey!"

When General Zachary Taylor of Jefferson County came home a hero from the Mexican-American War, the Whig Party wanted to run him for president.

A Whig bigwig told "the Hero of Buena Vista" that the nomination was his for the asking. The old soldier did not waste words on a reply. "Stop your nonsense and drink your whiskey!" he said, according to Boller's book, *Presidential Anecdotes*.

Dubbed "Old Rough and Ready" by his troops who idolized him, Taylor changed his mind. He got elected in 1848 but died suddenly in office in 1850. He was sixty-five.

Though Taylor was living in Louisiana when he was elected president, he grew up in Jefferson County, where he was buried. Taylor's tomb is the

Zachary Taylor. *Courtesy of the Kentucky Historical Society.*

The Texas Revolution and the Mexican-American War

Taylor monument. *Courtesy of the author.*

A stone likeness of Taylor tops his monument. *Courtesy of the author.*

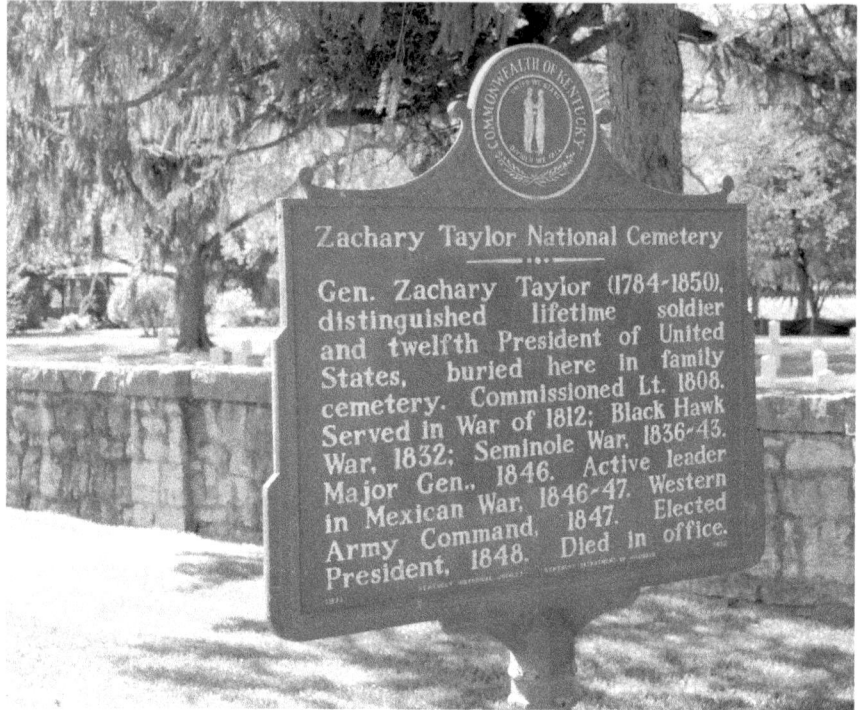

State historical society marker at the entrance to the Zachary Taylor National Cemetery. *Courtesy of the author.*

best-known grave site in Zachary Taylor National Cemetery in Louisville. The 16.5-acre military burial ground is at 4710 Brownsboro Road, three blocks west of the Watterson Expressway. "A lot of people probably didn't know our twelfth president was buried in Louisville until there was all that business about exhuming his body in 1991 to see if he had been murdered," said Gary Peak, cemetery director.

For the record, Taylor died of natural causes.

The president and his wife, Margaret Smith Taylor, are interred in a stone mausoleum the federal government built for the first couple in 1926. The Taylors were moved from an old family vault that is nearby.

The presidential crypt is shadowed by a thirty-five-foot shaft topped by a marble statue of Taylor in a general's uniform. The president's reputed last words are chiseled on the monument's base: "I have endeavored to do my duty, I am ready to die."

The State of Kentucky erected the monument in 1883, thirty-five years after naming Taylor County for the soldier-president. Two other states

The Texas Revolution and the Mexican-American War

claim Taylor as a presidential son: Virginia, where he was born in 1784, and Louisiana, where he also lived.

But Taylor considered Kentucky his official home, according to the *Kentucky Encyclopedia*. Lewis and Richard Collins's old *History of Kentucky* explained that Taylor "was brought by his parents to the State when only nine months old, and received his first impressions of the world amid the hearty hunters, the tall forests and romantic scenery of the dark and bloody ground."

In 1785, Taylor's father and Revolutionary War veteran, Colonel Richard Taylor, migrated to Kentucky, settling on a farm he called Springfield. Son Zachary opted for a military career.

By the time the Mexican-American War broke out, Taylor was a veteran army man. He had soldiered in the War of 1812 and the Seminole Wars.

At Buena Vista, the Mexicans under Santa Anna outnumbered Taylor and his troops nearly four to one. "Calm, collected, and resolved, he rose superior to the danger of his situation, and wrested victory from defeat," according to the Collins history book. "It is admitted by all who were present, that no man but General Taylor could have won the victory of Buena Vista."

A hard fighter on the battlefield, Taylor hated parade ground spit and polish. His statue to the contrary, Taylor seldom wore a uniform in the Mexican-American War. He preferred a battered straw hat and plain civilian clothes. One officer said Old Rough and Ready looked less like a general and "more like a farmer going to market with eggs to sell," according to *Presidential Anecdotes*.

Many northern Whigs opposed the Mexican-American War. They claimed that President James K. Polk, a southern slave-owning Democrat, provoked the war to grab Mexican territory he could turn into more slave states.

Though Taylor was the war's top general, the Whig brass opted for practical politics over principle. They figured he would be a shoo-in for president in 1848. An admirer predicted the general would win by "spontaneous combustion."

It took votes, but Taylor triumphed.

Taylor had no political experience. But he topped a pair of veteran lawmakers—Clay and Senator Daniel Webster of Massachusetts—for the Whig nomination.

Taylor, too, was a slave owner. He also wanted to see the country grow. But he angered the proslavery South by supporting the admission of California as a free state in 1850.

In Congress, debate over California and the expansion of slavery heated up in the summer of that fateful year. Taylor took a day off on July 4 to attend cornerstone-laying ceremonies at the new Washington Monument.

It was hot as blue blazes; Taylor sat hatless in the sun. After the long program, he returned to the White House and tried to cool off. The president reputedly gobbled a bowl of raw vegetables or fruit, washing it down with iced milk.

He collapsed into bed with severe cramps, diarrhea and a burning fever. Doctors tried a variety of remedies, including bloodletting. Taylor suffered for five more days before he died.

The president's body rested in peace in Louisville until 1991, when it seemed like a real-life Agatha Christie novel was played out in the national cemetery. Clara Rising, a Florida author writing a book about Taylor, suggested that he might have been poisoned. She wondered if Old Rough and Ready's proslavery enemies might have spiked his food with deadly arsenic.

Rising convinced officials to exhume Taylor's body. Samples of the president's hair, fingernails, teeth and breastbone were dispatched to laboratories for examination by experts.

"The story got national—even international—coverage in the media," Peak said. "But the tests proved that President Taylor had definitely not died of arsenic poison."

The experts concluded that the president's doctors might have unwittingly killed him by employing cures worse than the complaint, or whatever he ate or drank may have been fatally contaminated by bacteria.

"Your Spirits Are in a Land of Peace and Rest"

The iron sphere atop Lawrenceburg's rare Mexican-American War monument looks like a cannonball.

"It's not," said John Trowbridge, command historian of the Kentucky National Guard, who helped restore the monument in 1997. "The ball was used in coal mines to break up the coal."

Trowbridge said a real cannonball surmounted the memorial when it was built on the Anderson County courthouse lawn in 1847.

"One of the soldiers brought it back from the war," he explained. "But somebody stole it. Tom Fugate, who has then [curator of]...the Kentucky Military History Museum, said he had some balls from coal mines that looked like cannonballs and he gave me one to use."

A group of ninety-two Anderson County men volunteered for the Mexican-American War. They mustered into service as Company C, Second Regiment of Foot.

The Texas Revolution and the Mexican-American War

Lawrence County's Mexican-American War memorial. *Courtesy of the author.*

After the conflict, monuments to Bluegrass State veterans sprouted in a handful of Kentucky communities, including Lawrenceburg. The men of Company C nicknamed themselves the Salt River Tigers.

Seven Tigers were killed and another seven were wounded in the Battle of Buena Vista, the outfit's only major combat action. Nine others perished, presumably from wounds or disease. The names of the dead soldiers are carved on the stone shaft.

Captain John H. McBrayer, who had commanded the Tigers, believed his men who had shed their blood in Mexico merited a monument. "He and others had it built in late 1847," Trowbridge said.

The monument faces Main Street. The inscription on the front side of the monument's base explains:

Hidden History of Kentucky Soldiers

*This monument
is erected by the
citizens of Anderson County
in honor of the valor and
sacrifice of the volunteers of
this county who served in the War with Mexico
1846–1848*

The right-side inscription says:

*The Salt River Tigers
of Anderson County
under Capt. John H. McBrayer
Company C, 2nd Regiment Kentucky Volunteer Infantry
Killed at the
Battle of Buena Vista
Fought on February 22–23, 1847
William Board, David Davis
James Johnson, James Layten
Arthur Thacker, John Watson
William P. Reynolds*

The left side says:

*Wounded
William R. Howard, Berry Perry
Joseph Montgomery, George Read
George Searcy, William Warford
William W. Lillard*

The back says:

*Died
in the Nation's service
T. Levy Driskell, John Hoffman
Thomas Gudgel, Chesley Hamlet
Peyton Brown, Carter Bryant
Henderson Wise, James Petty
Mark L. Leathers*

The Texas Revolution and the Mexican-American War

Departed and lamented patriots
There is something that whispers
That your spirits are in a land
of peace and rest

By the time the monument neared its sesquicentennial year, weathering had all but worn away the words carved into the stone. Five lines were illegible. A local Sons of Confederate Veterans group, which helped push for refurbishing the monument, tried to make them out.

"They never could," Trowbridge recalled.

He suspected somebody had written them down. Trowbridge's research turned up an old copy of the wording.

But his discovery came too late. "The SCV came up with their version and that was put on the monument," he said.

It reads:

The Laurels of Patriotism are
always green. Go, volunteers, to
any portion of this Union and some
eye will beam with recognition,
some tongue will pronounce your
valor and proclaim you the war
torn soldiers who bravely fought
at the Battle of Buena Vista.

The original words, according to Trowbridge, were:

They are gone—
Fathers and Mothers and Friends
may weep for them and yet be proud
that the terrors of the battlefield neither
sully their honor nor patriotism

Across the lawn from the Mexican-American War monument is a larger memorial to the county's Confederates, including another group of Salt River Tigers. They composed Company C of the Second Kentucky Confederate Infantry Regiment.

Anderson County, like almost all Kentucky counties, sent men to both sides in America's bloodiest war. Trowbridge likes to tell the story about the time a local Union Home Guard company paraded through the streets of Lawrenceburg.

"This Confederate sympathizer came out on his porch and started yelling and hollering insults at them," he said. The Home Guards promptly tossed him in jail.

The gent proved some old Tigers could still roar, according to Trowbridge. "He was Captain Thomas McBrayer."

Chapter 4

FENIANS AND CUSTER'S "NEXT-TO-LAST STAND" AND LAST STAND

"DONE AS BEST WE COULD"

Louisville potter-politician Patrick Bannon didn't aim to help unify Canada. The Irish-born Bannon and others in the Fenian Brotherhood schemed to seize America's northern neighbor and hold it hostage for a free Ireland.

The post–Civil War plot backfired. Britain's Canadian colonies banded together partly because of the Fenians, Irish Americans opposed to British rule in their homeland. Between 1866 and 1871, small Fenian groups raided Canadian territory from New Brunswick to Manitoba.

Bannon, a native of County Down, Ireland, immigrated to Louisville, where he operated terra cotta factories. He apparently served on the city council, too.

Bannon, a Fenian "senator," helped recruit the Seventeenth Kentucky Infantry Regiment, mostly from Louisville's Irish American community. Many of the volunteers fought on the Union side in the Civil War.

"There were several Fenians from the Irish populations of Kentucky, Tennessee and Midwestern states in the Fenian raids," said David J. Bertuca, map librarian at the University of Buffalo, New York. "Some of the top leaders were from Kentucky and Tennessee."

The Seventeenth Kentucky was part of a Fenian band in 1866 that whipped Canadian militia and British redcoats at the Battle of Ridgeway, Ontario. The Fenians soon retreated to Buffalo, New York.

Bannon didn't fight in the battle. Colonel George Owen Starr, Lieutenant Colonel John Spalding (also spelled "Spaulding") and Captain Michael Bolands—all of Louisville—and Captain John A. Geary of Lexington led the Seventeenth Kentucky, according to the 155th New York Volunteer Infantry Re-Enactor Regiment's website.

"It made sense to involve guys like Spalding, who was a Civil War veteran," said Jim Holmberg, curator of special collections at the Filson Historical Society in Louisville. Spalding was a captain in the Fifteenth Kentucky Union Infantry. The regiment fought at the Battles of Perryville in Kentucky as well as Stones River, Tennessee, Chickamauga, Georgia, and in the Atlanta campaign.

Bolands was a sergeant in the 10th Kentucky Union Cavalry. He was wounded at the Battle of Ridgeway and captured, according to the 115th New York Re-Enactors.

Bannon returned home, dejected. "Our men were made into a forlorn hope—some in prison, some in strange locales wounded, and some killed," he lamented in a letter. "We have no plan nor programme to follow. Done as best we could, thought we were doing right but probably done all wrong, for all we know."

The Fenian raids don't rate much ink in American history books. They are better chronicled north of the border. "In 1867, alarmed by the Fenian raids and seeking mutual defence against the continuing American threat, the province of Canada, divided into Ontario and Quebec, joined New Brunswick and Nova Scotia in the new Dominion of Canada, a self-governing British colony," according to WarMuseum.ca, the website of the Canadian War Museum in Ottawa, Canada's capital.

Custer's "Next-to-Last Stand"

Few episodes in the history of the old West are better known than Custer's Last Stand.

"We say his next-to-last stand was in Elizabethtown," Twylane Van Lahr declared.

Van Lahr is director of the red brick Brown-Pusey House, a library and history center that was Lieutenant Colonel George Armstrong Custer's local headquarters in 1871–1873. "Custer and his wife, Elizabeth, lived in a cottage on the property," she explained.

Fenians and Custer's "Next-to-Last Stand" and Last Stand

After the Civil War, Custer and two companies of his Seventh Cavalry Regiment were sent to Elizabethtown, the Hardin County seat, to break up the Ku Klux Klan and put local moonshiners out of business. Off duty, Custer found time to buy and race horses, hunt with his prize hound dogs and dabble in Elizabethtown society.

"He apparently enjoyed himself while he was here," Van Lahr said. "But his wife apparently did not."

The town belles supposedly were smitten with the dashing young colonel. "Perhaps that is one of the reasons why Mrs. Custer wasn't very fond of Elizabethtown," Van Lahr said. "She wrote letters complaining about the muddy streets and about hogs roaming wild in town. We weren't sophisticated enough for Mrs. Custer."

Since then, the streets have been paved, and swine no longer wander freely in Elizabethtown. But the Custer connection is cited at the Brown-Pusey House, which is operated by a private, not-for-profit foundation.

A metal state historical marker out front tells about Custer and Elizabethtown.

"We have a coffee server that the Custers likely would have used," Van Lahr said. "There's also a grandfather clock that was in the house when they were here. An original photo of Custer and two books from his personal library are on display."

The flamboyant, Ohio-born Custer, who liked to wear his blond hair long and who designed his own flashy uniforms, was a famous Civil War soldier and Indian fighter before he arrived in Elizabethtown. An 1861 West Point graduate, he was one of the war's youngest generals, earning brevet brigadier's stars at age twenty-three.

Later, he was promoted to brevet major general for bravery in battle. The army did not need as many generals after the war, so his rank was reduced to lieutenant colonel. The army sent him out West to battle the Sioux and Cheyenne.

The fact that Custer had been a Yankee did not seem to hurt his popularity in generally prosouthern Elizabethtown, according to Van Lahr. "He and his wife were invited to many parties and he often went hunting with important local people."

But in *Boots and Saddles, or Life in Dakota with General Custer*, her book about her husband, "Libby" Custer said little about Elizabethtown except that Lieutenant Colonel Custer found soldiering here "very disagreeable." She explained that "a true cavalryman feels that a life in the saddle on the free open plain is his legitimate existence."

Custer returned to the West with recruits and horses from Kentucky. He and many of his men were killed on June 25, 1876, at the Battle of the Little Bighorn River in Montana, popularly known as Custer's Last Stand. (Surviving troopers fought into June 26, when the battle ended.)

Custer's "next-to-last stand" is reenacted from time to time in Elizabethtown as part of an outdoor theater program. Charlie Skees, a retired high school history teacher, plays Custer.

Kentuckian's Medal of Honor Was in a Movie

Custer's Last Stand produced two dozen Medal of Honor winners, including four Kentuckians. One of them, Private William M. Harris of Madison County, is buried at Camp Nelson National Cemetery in Jessamine County.

Besides Harris, Privates George D. Scott of Garrard County and Thomas W. Stivers, another Madison Countian, plus Saddler Sergeant Otto Voit of

Harris's tombstone. *Courtesy of the author.*

Fenians and Custer's "Next-to-Last Stand" and Last Stand

Water Carrier Ravine. *Courtesy of the author.*

Louisville, won the nation's highest award for valor. Custer lost his life, about 40 percent of his men and the battle.

A state historical marker in Richmond, the Madison County seat, tells about the heroism of Harris, Scott and Stivers. It does not mention the German-born Voit.

Several other horsemen from Kentucky rode with Custer and his storied Seventh Cavalry. On June 25, 1876, he attacked eight thousand to ten thousand Sioux, Cheyenne and Arapaho—including about two thousand warriors—who were camped at the Little Bighorn.

Custer had 647 soldiers, plus a few armed civilians and white and Native American scouts. He and 262 troopers—including all 209 who charged with him—were killed, most of them on the first day of the two-day battle.

Major Marcus Reno, Captain Frederick Benteen and the rest of the Seventh Cavalry were driven back, too. They ended up trying to hold off the Indians on a grassy hilltop above the shallow river.

June 26 was another hot, dry day. Every canteen was empty. Benteen feared many of the wounded would perish without water. He called for volunteers to run a gauntlet of Indian rifle fire and arrows to fetch the lifesaving liquid.

Harris, Scott, Stivers and sixteen other men agreed to go. Lugging canteens, cook pots and kettles, they returned with the precious water in about twenty minutes. Their route is known as Water Carrier Ravine. The gully is part of the Little Bighorn Battlefield National Monument near Crow Agency, Montana.

With the approach of more soldiers, the Indians retreated on the evening of June 26. All nineteen troopers survived to win the Medal of Honor. Harris died in 1895. In 1999, his remains were reinterred at Camp Nelson National Cemetery. A special Medal of Honor tombstone marks his grave.

Stivers was never presented his Medal of Honor, though a special Medal of Honor tombstone commemorates his place of burial in the Richmond city cemetery. Harris and Scott apparently did not receive their medals either. Voit, who lived in Louisville, where he died in 1906 at age sixty-one, apparently got his medal.

"Stivers, Harris and Scott were discharged from the army on August 5, 1876, in Montana Territory," Trowbridge said. "They (and Voit, who stayed in the army until 1880) weren't awarded the Medal of Honor until October 5, 1878."

The army never found Stivers, Harris and Scott to give them their medals. "Stivers and Harris, who were cousins, returned to Madison County," Trowbridge said. "What became of Scott is unknown." He was from Garrard County.

Stivers was dead by the time his Medal of Honor was approved. He was gunned down in 1877 at Whit Moody's bawdyhouse near Richmond, where he worked. Harris died in a Berea shootout eight years later. He was thirty-five.

Trouble brewed between Stivers, twenty-seven, and George Moody, Whit's young son, when he came to collect the rent. Stivers refused to pay him, according to the *Lexington Daily Press*.

The "big bully," according to the newspaper, "abused the youth by pulling his ears and slapping his face." Stivers slammed Moody "against a wall…and kicked him." The boy pulled a small pistol and fatally shot Stivers, the *Press* reported.

Fenians and Custer's "Next-to-Last Stand" and Last Stand

After an "examining trial," Moody was acquitted in the slaying of the Little Bighorn hero, the *Press* said. Long after Stivers, Harris and Scott were gone, John Ford, the famous Hollywood director, heard about their unclaimed medals, which were at the War Department in Washington. He wanted one as a prop for his movie, *Fort Apache*.

Ford, an Academy Award winner who directed many Westerns, managed to get Stivers's old medal for his new film, which premiered in 1948.

Ward Bond, a familiar character actor, played Sergeant Major Michael O'Rourke in *Fort Apache*. The Irish-born O'Rourke was supposed to be a veteran horse soldier who earned the Medal of Honor, the military's highest award for valor, in the Civil War.

"Bond wore Stivers's medal on camera before Ford found out that was illegal," Trowbridge said. "After that, he wore a copy. But copying a Medal of Honor is illegal, too. If you watch the movie, it's impossible to tell in which scenes Bond is wearing the real medal or the copy."

Trowbridge said an Indiana collector has Stivers's Medal of Honor. Trowbridge helped get a new Medal of Honor for Harris's descendants and assisted in the trooper's reburial at the Camp Nelson National Cemetery near Nicholasville, the Jessamine County seat. Harris's grave also has a Medal of Honor tombstone.

Thanks in part to Trowbridge, a Medal of Honor memorial in the city cemetery at Lancaster, the Garrard County seat, honors Scott.

"I have no idea what happened to Scott's or Harris's original Medals of Honor," Trowbridge said.

"A Sergeant of Excellent Character"

Saddler Michael P. Madden gulped brandy before an army surgeon amputated his right leg during the Battle of the Little Bighorn.

The sawbones gave the Irish-born Kentucky enlistee another snort afterward. "Supposedly, Madden was so appreciative of the second drink that he told the surgeon, 'Doctor, cut off me other leg,'" said Bob Reece, president of the Friends of the Little Bighorn Battlefield, a nonprofit group.

Madden, a Civil War veteran, rejoined the army at Louisville in 1871. It evidently is not known if Madden was living in Louisville. He had been discharged at Mount Vernon, Kentucky, according to Reece.

Madden was one of the water carriers. He did not receive a Medal of Honor but earned sergeant's stripes "for distinguished bravery in action."

After a rifle slug hit Madden, forty, in the right leg, just above the ankle, Dr. Henry R. Porter braved a storm of Indian gunfire to amputate the trooper's mangled limb. The twenty-eight-year-old civilian physician under contract to the army reputedly used a collapsed tent for a ground cover and operating table.

E.A. Brininstool included Madden's legendary quip in his book, *Troopers with Custer: Historic Incidents of the Battle of the Little Big Horn*. The author quoted Private William Slaper, another water carrier: "Before amputating…the surgeon gave Mike a stiff horn of brandy to brace him up. Mike went through the ordeal without a whimper, and was given another drink. Smacking his lips in appreciation, he whispered to the surgeon, 'Doctor, cut off me other leg!'"

Madden was placed on a litter and evacuated by mule. Once, the cantankerous critter balked and sent its human cargo thudding to the ground. Madden, who apparently suffered no further injury, eventually went by Bighorn River steamboat to Fort Lincoln, North Dakota, where he recovered.

The army discharged him in August 1876 "as a sergeant of excellent character." Madden's date of death is apparently unknown, but he may be buried in the Fort Snelling National Cemetery in Minneapolis.

"Die If Need Be with Your Face to the Foe!"

The army left only one soldier buried where he fell at the battle of the Little Bighorn.

His father, a Civil War hero from a famous Kentucky family, asked that his son's grave be undisturbed. "I know of no more fitting place for my son to be buried than on the very ground where he fought and died like a man, with his face to the foe," Colonel Thomas L. Crittenden said.

The army agreed. From 1876 to 1931, Lieutenant John Jordan Crittenden's remains stayed on the grassy hill where he died.

In 1931, Crittenden was reburied in Custer National Cemetery beneath the old tombstone that marked his battlefield grave for more than fifty years. Next to the battlefield park, the cemetery contains graves of veterans of America's wars through Vietnam.

Crittenden perished in a hail of Indian bullets and arrows. An arrow shattered twenty-two-year-old Crittenden's glass eye.

The "handsome, manly boy" probably was dead already, according to John A. Doerner, chief historian at the park. Victorious Sioux, Cheyenne and Arapaho warriors stripped, scalped and otherwise mutilated the corpses of many soldiers.

Fenians and Custer's "Next-to-Last Stand" and Last Stand

Monument on Last Stand Hill that is inscribed with Crittenden's name. *Courtesy of the author.*

Soon after the battle, the army buried Custer and his slain men in shallow graves at or near where they fell on hilltops, hillsides and in ravines. Indian tepee poles marked each grave, Doerner said.

In 1877, the army reburied Custer at West Point, his alma mater. The bodies of eleven officers and two civilians who died with him also were sent east for reinterment in family plots or national cemeteries.

In 1881, the army erected an eighteen-ton stone obelisk to Custer and the Seventh Cavalry on Last Stand Hill, where Custer was killed. About 220 soldiers, scouts and civilians who died with Custer were reburied in a mass grave around the monument.

Thomas L. Crittenden's body remained on Calhoun Hill, named for his commander, Captain James Calhoun, Custer's brother-in-law. Lieutenant Colonel Crittenden sent a simple civilian tombstone for the lonely grave.

In those days, a veteran could have a military tombstone only if he was buried in a national cemetery, according to Jerry Cecil, of Winchester, a historian and writer. "But Colonel Crittenden's request that his son remained buried on the battlefield was right in line with the warrior ethic of the Crittenden family."

Crittenden was named for his grandfather, Senator John Jordan Crittenden. Although a War of 1812 veteran, the elder Crittenden was best known as a peacemaker. He authored the Crittenden Compromise, a last-minute effort to stave off the Civil War.

"Tragedy was no stranger to the Crittendens," said Ron Bryant, manager of the Waveland State Historic Site in Lexington. "Not only was Lieutenant Crittenden killed with Custer, his father and uncle [Confederate General George B. Crittenden] were on opposite sides in the Civil War."

Thomas L. Crittenden also made general in the nation's bloodiest conflict. He rejoined the army as a colonel afterward.

In 1890, the army put up regulation grave markers where Custer and each of his men had been buried, Doerner said. The white marble markers are scattered across the prairie grass, as if by the wind. (Since 1999, the National Park Service has erected three reddish-brown stone markers showing where Indian warriors fell.)

The names of Custer and all of his men who died at the Little Bighorn are chiseled into the Seventh Cavalry monument. "J.J. CRITTENDEN" is on the memorial.

Lieutenant Crittenden died far from home. Born in Frankfort in 1854, Crittenden enrolled at West Point in 1871. He flunked philosophy and failed to graduate, but the army made him a second lieutenant anyway in 1875.

That same year, Crittenden lost his left eye in a hunting accident, Doerner said. But the army deemed him fit enough to saddle up with Custer's storied regiment in 1876.

Like his father, Crittenden was a foot soldier. The army assigned the young lieutenant to the Twentieth Infantry out west. Perhaps seeking adventure, Crittenden volunteered for service in the saddle with the dashing Custer.

Thomas L. Crittenden saw his son off to what would be his first and last campaign in 1876. "My boy," the colonel reputedly admonished his son, "Do your duty! Never retreat! Die, if need be, with your face to the foe!"

After the battle, a surviving officer from one of the other battalions spied the bloody corpses of Calhoun, Crittenden and their troops sprawled in the prairie grass. "The bodies of these officers were lying a short distance in rear of their men, in the very place where they belonged, and the bodies of their men forming a very regular skirmish line," he wrote. "Crittenden's body was shot full of arrows."

After defeating Custer, the Indians scattered from the Little Bighorn, taking most of their dead. Other than the tepee poles the army turned into grave markers, the Indians left little behind.

Fenians and Custer's "Next-to-Last Stand" and Last Stand

The Indians also took many battle trophies, including a gold pocket watch. The timepiece ended up in Canada where Sitting Bull and a group of Sioux fled after the battle.

In 1880, a Canadian fur trader bought the watch from a man who was half-Native American and half-white. The man said he got the watch from a Sioux warrior, who claimed he took it from an officer he killed at the Little Bighorn.

Hoping to identify the officer, the trader wrote to the Liverpool, England firm that made the watch. He included the serial number, which enabled company officials to determine that Thomas L. Crittenden bought the watch in 1850.

The trader sent the watch to General William T. Sherman, who served with Crittenden in the Civil War. "I gave my watch to my son many years ago," the veteran soldier said. "I saw him start on the unfortunate expedition and know that he had his watch with him," Crittenden added. The rare relic is in the Kentucky History Center, operated by the state historical society in Frankfort.

It has been said that Crittenden's body was moved to make room for a new road through the national park. Cecil, who is also a retired army colonel, suggests another reason. "The superintendent of the national cemetery had apparently taken matters into his own hands after a letter was received 'complaining that the Custodian of the Custer Battlefield was not taking proper care of Lt. John Jordan Crittenden's grave,'" Cecil wrote in *Greasy Grass*, a magazine published yearly by the Custer Battlefield Historical and Museum Association.

At any rate, Lieutenant Crittenden was reburied on September 11, 1931, with full military honors, according to Cecil. Members of the American Legion post in nearby Hardin, Montana, provided the honor guard.

A military tombstone also marks Crittenden's old grave site, listing his name, rank, regiment and date of death. The civilian tombstone only tells Crittenden's name, birthday and death date.

Before the civilian tombstone arrived, the army marked the battlefield grave with a simple wooden cross. It was painted white with "JJ CRITTENDEN LIEUT 20 INFTY" on it in black capital letters.

"IT SEEMED A DEADLY, ENDLESS, HOPELESS RUN"

Trooper William David Nugent of the Seventh Cavalry remembered the "bullets singing and sighing all around."

The Native American horsemen, he recalled, charged from a choking cloud of dust, "flung up their carbines, took bobbing aim and fired. They made sudden dead-on runs at the column until their horses scraped against the running mounts of the troopers…Presently the column, pouring forward at a full run, was engaged in deadly hand-to-hand wrestling."

Nugent, twenty-three, of Leitchfield, the Grayson County seat, survived Custer's Last Stand. He earned a niche in *Two Centuries in Elizabethtown and Hardin County, Kentucky*, a book by Daniel Elmo McClure Jr. It includes Nugent's harrowing personal account of the Little Bighorn fight.

According to McClure, Nugent was nineteen when he joined Custer's regiment in Elizabethtown, which is near Leitchfield. Luckily for Nugent, he was not in Custer's ill-fated charge. He attacked and retreated with Reno. "It seemed a deadly, endless, hopeless run," Nugent said. "The battalion was a skeleton, its identity half buried in the smothering, close-riding Sioux; the horses ran in the loose gait of near exhaustion."

The Indians halted Reno's force after it crossed the Little Bighorn. As the cavalrymen spurred their horses back across the shallow river, some of the lead animals, "crazed by thirst, slackened and tore the reins free from the troopers' tight grasps. They stopped belly-deep in the stream and made a barricade which spread back and blocked the small pathway down the bluff."

In desperation, the horse soldiers dismounted and forded the river wherever they could as "carbine fire began to whip at the troopers in the water." Men still in the saddle tried to follow Reno up the grassy bluffs.

Nugent saw a hatless Reno "watching his broken battalion come up, with a gray, dazed expression on his face. He kept saying, 'Spread out and cover the others.' One by one the troopers reached the crest and fell in their tracks."

Nugent volunteered to be a water carrier. But like Madden, he did not receive a Medal of Honor.

Bending over the stream and filling a canteen, he felt a sharp blow on his forehead. Wiping away blood, he figured a bullet had grazed him.

A canteen cork had beaned him. An Indian round hit a canteen floating in the water. The impact popped the stopper against Nugent's skull.

Survivors in Nugent's company included two men from Hardin County, John S. Ragsdale and John J. Thomas. They, too, had joined Custer in Elizabethtown.

Nugent and Thomas settled out west. Ragsdale, according to McClure, returned to Elizabethtown after he left the army. Ragsdale claimed he was in Custer's charge and had "feigned death on the battlefield and thus escaped the massacre," McClure wrote, adding that nobody believed Ragsdale.

CHAPTER 5

TO THE SPANISH-AMERICAN WAR

"A 'SLAVERY' FROM WHICH WE ARE EMANCIPATING HIM"

Sergeant Brent Woods did not know he was riding into a valley of death.

Apache warriors ambushed Woods's small cavalry patrol and a handful of cowboys at Gavilan Canyon, New Mexico, on August 19, 1881. Trapped in the dusty, dry gorge, the column seemed doomed.

Though wounded, Woods led what was left of his men in a charge that forced the Apaches to flee. His heroism earned him a Medal of Honor.

Born a slave in Pulaski County, Woods is apparently one of only two African Americans from Kentucky to win the nation's highest medal for valor. (The other was Sergeant Andrew Jackson Smith, a Civil War soldier.) Woods is buried in Mill Springs National Cemetery, near Nancy.

"He's pretty well known here now," said Louann Hardy, reference librarian at the Pulaski County Library in Somerset, the county seat. That was not always so.

"For years, he was buried in an old abandoned cemetery in Somerset," Hardy said. "He was all but forgotten."

Woods was reinterred with full military honors at the national cemetery named for the nearby Civil War Battle of Mill Springs. The epitaph chiseled into Woods's two-foot, white marble military tombstone identifies him as a Medal of Honor recipient.

Woods's Medal of Honor tombstone. *Courtesy of the author.*

Woods rode in the Ninth Cavalry, a black regiment sent west to fight Indians after the Civil War. Such African American troops were known as Buffalo Soldiers.

Woods was eighteen years old when he left Pulaski County for the army in 1873. He was sent to Wyoming and assigned to Company B of the Ninth Cavalry.

In the summer of 1881, Woods's outfit was in New Mexico, battling Chief Nana and his band of Apaches. The Indians had been waging a small but bloody guerrilla war against whites encroaching on Apache territory.

When it looked like Nana and his warriors planned to slip across the border into Mexico, the army dispatched a lieutenant and seventeen troopers, including Sergeant Woods, to stop them. About twenty ranchers rode along as reinforcements.

Nana's force attacked and pinned the troopers and ranchers down as they entered sun-baked, high-walled Gavilan Canyon. Six troopers, including the lieutenant, died in a hail of Apache bullets.

Determined to rescue as many men as he could, Woods took command. First, he ran a gauntlet of Indian rifle fire to lead the ranchers out of the valley of death. Dodging more gunshots, he returned, dismounted and led the surviving troopers in a foot charge. A biographical sketch of Woods in the Pulaski County Library tells what happened next:

> *In advance of his men, Sergeant Woods fought his way to a high ridge and from there conducted a one man war against the Indians, eventually driving them from their position. A bullet grazed his arm but Sergeant Woods shot with such accuracy and speed that the Indian advance and a retreat followed.*

In 1882, Nana surrendered to white authorities, but Woods did not get his Medal of Honor until 1894. Another Buffalo Soldier remembered that, at Gavilan Canyon, the sergeant's "energy and skill defeated the Indians and saved the detachment from an entire massacre."

Woods retired from the army in 1902. He moved back to Somerset, where he died in 1906 and was buried in a pauper's grave in an old church cemetery, according to Hardy. In 1983, his remains were removed to the national cemetery.

At a special memorial service in 1984, Representative Hal Rogers of Somerset eulogized the old Buffalo Soldier. "Just as it was a terrible blight for Brent Woods to have lived in slavery, so too would it have been an injustice for his heroism to have been forever forgotten, a 'slavery' from which we are emancipating him today," the Washington lawmaker said.

"All I Want to Be Is Jailer of Letcher County"

It might be Kentucky's most famous political yarn.

Teddy Roosevelt leads the Rough Riders to victory at San Juan Hill. No sooner do the guns fall silent than he cuts a deal for the presidency with a potential rival, Corporal Fess Whitaker of Letcher County.

"This is going to make one of us president one day," Teddy tells Fess. The teenage trooper agrees and then concedes the White House to his colonel. "All I want to be is jailer of Letcher County," Fess demurs.

A Republican, Whitaker was elected jailer and judge of Letcher County. He told and retold the Teddy Roosevelt tale on the stump in Whitesburg, the county seat, and elsewhere local voters gathered.

"Kentucky politicians told the story for years," Klotter said. "Of course, it's not true. But it does show how important local politics was to people. It also says something about what politicians will say to win elections."

Fess was in the army during the Spanish-American War of 1898. Roosevelt, president from 1901 to 1909, was the conflict's great hero. The Battle of San Juan Hill, near Santiago, Cuba, grabbed headlines.

Whitaker was a cook who got no closer to combat than Florida, according to Klotter. Fess did serve with the Rough Riders, the historian added.

Nonetheless, Fess swore he took a Spanish slug at San Juan Hill. In *History of Corporal Fess Whitaker*, his 1918 autobiography, the jailer-judge explained:

> *Teddy, without a wound and I with a bullet wound in my left arm, took me by the hand and said: "Fess: we have gained a great battle for our country. You or I will be the next President of the United States, and if you get the nomination I am for you, and if I get the nomination I want you to be for me, for you have great influence in the United States."*

Eventually, the myth of Fess Whitaker became a staple in the story bag of Kentucky politicians, Republicans and Democrats.

Fess was elected county jailer in 1917, but in 1921, he ran afoul of Judge Sam Collins, a fellow Republican. Collins was a teetotaler; Whitaker enjoyed strong drink, according to Harry M. Caudill's book, *The Mountain, the Miner and the Lord.*

One day, Fess showed up tipsy in Collins's courtroom, so the judge jailed the jailer in his own lockup. Meanwhile, Collins had decided against another term in 1921. To get even, Whitaker tossed his hat in the ring against Collins's choice to be the new judge.

Large crowds began gathering at the jail to hear inmate Whitaker speak. Alarmed, Collins waded through one throng, hoping to talk Whitaker into bowing out, Caudill wrote.

When Fess threatened to douse Collins with a pitcher of buttermilk, the judge fled, but Whitaker caught him. The crowd watched as Whitaker declared, "John the Baptist baptized with water and Jesus Christ baptized with the Holy Ghost, but I am going to baptize you with buttermilk!" The multitude roared with approval when Fess emptied the pitcher's contents on Collins's head, according to Caudill.

Nonetheless, Collins—ever after "Buttermilk Sam"—went home, put on dry clothes and charged Whitaker with assault and battery. Still behind bars on election day, Fess won. "Jailed Jailer Elected Judge of Letcher County," Caudill quoted the *Louisville Courier-Journal* headline.

After the governor pardoned him, Whitaker tried to "baptize" Collins with buttermilk again. But the ex-judge was nowhere to be found, Caudill wrote.

Fess's fable survived long after a car crash cut his life short in 1927. Whitaker was forty-seven.

CHAPTER 6

WORLD WAR I

KENTUCKY'S "ANSWER" TO SERGEANT YORK

"The most modest hero of the world war" is buried in Louisville's Zachary Taylor National Cemetery.

That hero, Sergeant Willie Sandlin, was Kentucky's only Medal of Honor winner in World War I.

The Leslie Countian single-handedly wiped out three German machine gun nests, killed at least twenty-four enemy soldiers and reputedly helped capture two hundred more in France in 1918.

A grateful France also rewarded Sandlin with its highest honor for bravery in war, the Military Medal. But the Kentuckian was so publicity shy that he would not wear his medals home.

Willie Sandlin died in 1949 at age fifty-nine. He succumbed to a lung ailment attributed to a German poison gas attack.

Sandlin was twenty-eight when General John J. Pershing awarded him the Medal of Honor, America's highest decoration for valor. Born near Buckhorn in Perry County in 1890, he grew up in Leslie County, where he was living when he joined the army.

Sandlin arrived on France's blood-soaked Western Front in time for the great Allied offensive that finally defeated war-weary Germany. But on September 26, 1918, the enemy had enough fight left to stop Sandlin's outfit, the Thirty-third Division, near Bois de Forges, France.

Willie Sandlin. *Courtesy of the University of Louisville Archives.*

Sandlin's Medal of Honor tombstone. *Courtesy of the author.*

World War I

German machine guns had killed or wounded many of Sandlin's mates. Survivors were flat on their bellies, ducking the deadly hail of German fire.

But something made Willie Sandlin stand up. Armed with a rifle, automatic pistol and four hand grenades, the Kentuckian charged eight Germans in a machine gun nest.

"He showed conspicuous gallantry in action by advancing alone directly on a machinegun nest which was holding up the line with its fire," Sandlin's Medal of Honor citation reads. "He killed the crew with a grenade and enabled the line to advance. Later in the day he attacked alone and put out of action 2 other machinegun nests, setting a splendid example of bravery and coolness to his men."

Pershing, commander of the American Expeditionary Force in France, also noted Sandlin's bravery. He praised the Kentuckian for "conspicuous gallantry and intrepidity above and beyond the call of duty."

Sandlin never bragged about his brave feat. But his fellow Kentuckians dubbed him the Bluegrass State's "answer" to Sergeant Alvin C. York, the famous Tennessee Medal of Honor winner. York inspired the movie *Sergeant York*, a Hollywood classic that starred Gary Cooper.

A 1950 Lexington newspaper story called Sandlin "the most modest hero of the World War" and claimed he helped capture 200 Germans. York killed 28 enemy soldiers and captured 132.

After World War I, Sandlin settled on a farm on Owls Nest Creek, near Hyden, the Leslie County seat. He was buried in Hurricane Cemetery between Hyden and Wooten. After her husband's death, Belvia Sandlin moved to Louisville.

In 1990, she had her spouse's body reinterred in the national cemetery. She died in 1999 at age ninety-six and was buried next to him.

Sergeant Sandlin was not forgotten in Hyden, where he was a state highway department supervisor when he died. A Kentucky Historical Society marker on the courthouse lawn commemorates "Sgt. Willie Sandlin Only Kentuckian to receive the Congressional Medal of Honor in World War I."

An ordinary soldier's headstone marks Sandlin's grave in the 16.5-acre burial ground. But his name is etched on the stone in gold letters. A likeness of the Medal of Honor is also outlined in gold.

There is no mention of the Military Medal. Sandlin might not have minded if the Medal of Honor emblem had been left off, too.

"Like Chasing Rabbits Back Home"

Andrew Carman of Graves County saw no man's land only once.

"It looked like an old broom sedge field," said Carman, who farmed east of Mayfield, the county seat. "Nothing was growing. The ground was all torn up.

"There was barbed wire coiled up and some lower down to the ground. It looked like an old field somebody had just thrown away."

It was a killing field where Private Carman, twenty-three, almost died, charging the German enemy on the day Sandlin earned the Medal of Honor. "I don't know how long it was until I got hit by shrapnel," Carman said. "I went down and when I came to, I could feel blood all over my face and my left knee was hurting."

Though knocked unconscious, he pulled through.

Carman was entitled to sew a yellow wound stripe on the sleeve of his uniform. But in 1981, he decided he wanted a Purple Heart medal, which

Andrew Carman. *Courtesy of the author.*

Andrew Carman's grave marker. *Courtesy of the author.*

the army revived in 1932. "When I wrote the army about it, I said I just wanted to wear it a little while before I died," said Carman.

The shell that wounded Carman killed two of his mates in the storied 369th U.S. Infantry, an African American regiment mainly recruited from Harlem in New York City. Carman and the rest of the 3rd Battalion, seven hundred strong, rushed the Germans. Six hundred were killed or wounded.

Already, the 369th was famous for bravery in battle. They were nicknamed the Harlem Hellfighters and the Black Rattlers. It has been said that the 369th was in combat longer than any other American outfit in World War I.

Most white American generals did not want black combat troops. So they sent them to fight in French armies or used them as laborers.

Spurned by the American army brass, the 369th fought under French commanders who showered the men with praise and medals. The first two U.S. doughboys to win the coveted French Croix-de-Guerre with Star and Gold Palm were Sergeant Henry Johnson and Private Needham Roberts of the 369th. "He was a good-sized man and pretty quiet," said Carman of Johnson.

After the war ended in 1918, Carman traveled to the Rhine River with the 369th. He brought home a small brown pebble he picked up from the riverbank.

Carman was drafted in 1917 and went through basic training at segregated Camp Zachary Taylor in Louisville. Segregation and race discrimination were the law and the social order in Kentucky.

He shipped overseas from Newport News, Virginia, in a troopship convoy. Like thousands of other soldiers—white and African American—he was plagued by seasickness. "I was too sick to die," he said, grinning.

He said he might have perished if not for fellow Graves Countian Granual Whittemore. He coaxed Carman to eat to stay alive.

"I'd chew something, swallow it and it would come right back up. But he forced me to keep trying to eat and I made it."

After fourteen days at sea, Carman's ship docked at Brest, France. He was surprised when French soldiers and civilians treated him as an equal. "Segregation and prejudice, I didn't see any of that," he said. "The French treated me like a man. They treated me better than I'd ever been treated in my own country."

Like other African American troops handed over to the French army, Carman had to exchange his deadly accurate Springfield rifle for a French Lebel, a much inferior weapon. "We nicknamed them 'Lilly-Belles,'" he said.

Carman reached the front on the night of September 25. He found shelter in a trench dugout just as the French artillery opened fire. "You could look out of the ends of the dugout and see nothing but flame and fire from the big guns," he said.

Just before daybreak, the troops were ordered to prepare for battle. Carman waited in the trench for the command to go "over the top."

When it came after daylight, the men swarmed into the open, dashing across no man's land "like chasing rabbits back home," Carman said. But the quarry shot back.

After Carman regained consciousness, he tried to crawl back to his trench for medical aid. A German machine gunner pinned him down.

"Every time I tried to move, it was peck, peck, peck, peck. The bullets would hit all around me."

Finally, the German picked another target, giving Carman a chance to crawl away. He did.

"I was in the hospital when this captain came around and asked me if I was ready to go back to the front and I said I was," Carman recalled. "He asked me how many Huns I'd get him and I said twenty-four—twenty-three privates and an officer. He laughed and said, 'We need you.'"

World War I

Carman said when he got back to G Company, Third Battalion, he discovered he was the only man left from his squad. "There were eight other men, and I never did know what happened to them—if they were killed or wounded or transferred, or what."

Despite staggering losses, the 369th had shoved the Germans back on September 26. The regiment advanced ten miles.

The army discharged Carman in 1919. "Before I left, they gave me a wound stripe. They said a medal would come later."

Carman said he did not know what kind of medal to expect. "But I was proud to get the Purple Heart."

He credited the Mayfield Red Cross chapter with helping him get the decoration, which was pinned to the lapel of his suit coat in which he was buried. Carman died in 1983 at age eighty-eight. His widow kept the medal.

Another Kentucky "Black Rattler"

Rufus Ballard Atwood came home a war hero, but not to a hero's welcome in Hickman, his hometown.

Pomp Atwood feared for his son's safety, so he warned him to be in civilian clothes. Some other World War I veterans like Rufus Atwood had been cursed and beaten when they came home in uniform, according to his sister.

They were African American.

Atwood made sergeant in the 369th Infantry and won a Bronze Star for bravery. But he is better known as an educator. He earned three college degrees and served as president of historically African American Kentucky State College—now Kentucky State University—in Frankfort from 1929 to 1962. He was dean of agriculture at Prairie View State College in Texas from 1923 until he became president of Kentucky State.

Because Rufus Atwood's skin was black, he was treated as a second-class citizen in Hickman, where he was born in 1897. Atwood was afraid to don his army outfit until he was inside his wood-frame house, according to his sister, Anna Parker Atwood Hale. She said she never forgot the cruel reception African American World War I veterans received in Hickman, an old Mississippi River port and the Fulton County seat. (Whites in other Kentucky communities also mistreated African American veterans.)

"Black men put their lives on the line and fought for their country, too," said Hale, who was past ninety-five when she died. "I'll let the Lord take care of that."

Rufus Ballard Atwood.
Courtesy of the Kentucky State University Archives.

The Lord, she added, watched over Rufus Atwood. He received bachelor's degrees from Fisk University in Nashville and Iowa State University. Atwood added a master's degree from the University of Chicago.

He died in 1983 at age eighty-six and was buried in the Frankfort Cemetery. But the story of Atwood's heroism in World War I lives at the Warren Thomas Black History Museum, which is housed in Hickman's Thomas Chapel CME Church. Ex-slaves built the little house of worship in 1890.

Atwood was a student at Fisk when he volunteered for the army in 1918. Like Carman, Atwood had to endure rampant racism in the military.

After the war, historians largely ignored African Americans who went "over there" or minimized their role in the Allied victory. Long after the war, John Hope Franklin cited Atwood's heroism in his 1947 book, *From Slavery to Freedom: A History of American Negroes.*

World War I

Atwood won his Bronze Star on November 10, 1918, the day before World War I ended. "A shell struck the house in which the switchboard was being operated at Point-a-Mousson," Franklin wrote. "Sergeant Rufus B. Atwood rendered valuable assistance in reconstructing the switchboard and connecting new lines under heavy shell fire."

Franklin quoted from the official army report of Atwood's bravery:

> *When the ammunition dump began to explode in the same neighborhood, he remained on the job, tapping new connections. After repairs were made from the first explosion, there were two to follow which completely wrecked the switchboard room and tore out all the lines which were newly fixed. Sergeant Atwood was left alone, and he established a new switchboard and the same connections they had at first. The coolness with which he went about his work and the initiative he took in handling the situation justifies his being mentioned in orders.*

In 1962, Atwood became the first African American awarded the University of Kentucky's Algernon Sidney Sullivan Citizen Medallion for dedicating his life "to the education of young people and…for the advancement of interracial relations," according to the Kentucky Commission on Human Rights.

"The First American Soldier Who Made the Supreme Sacrifice"

Corporal James Bethel Gresham doesn't rate much ink in history books, though he was the first American killed in combat in World War I, according to a bronze plaque in the Evansville, Indiana cemetery where he is buried.

A pair of state historical markers in his native western Kentucky makes the same claim. "He was not as famous as Sgt. York or Willie Sandlin, but he was among the many native Kentuckians who bravely served in the trenches of World War I," said Bill Bright, curator at the Kentucky Military History Museum.

Gresham, whose life ended at age twenty-four, was not forgotten in McLean County, Kentucky, where he was born, or in Evansville, where he grew up. The highway bridge that spans the Green River between Rumsey and Calhoun, the McLean County seat, is named for the war hero. The James Bethel Gresham Memorial Home, a gift to his near-penniless mother from grateful citizens, still stands in Evansville.

James Bethel Gresham's tombstone. *Courtesy of the author.*

Gresham memorial flagpole. *Courtesy of the author.*

World War I

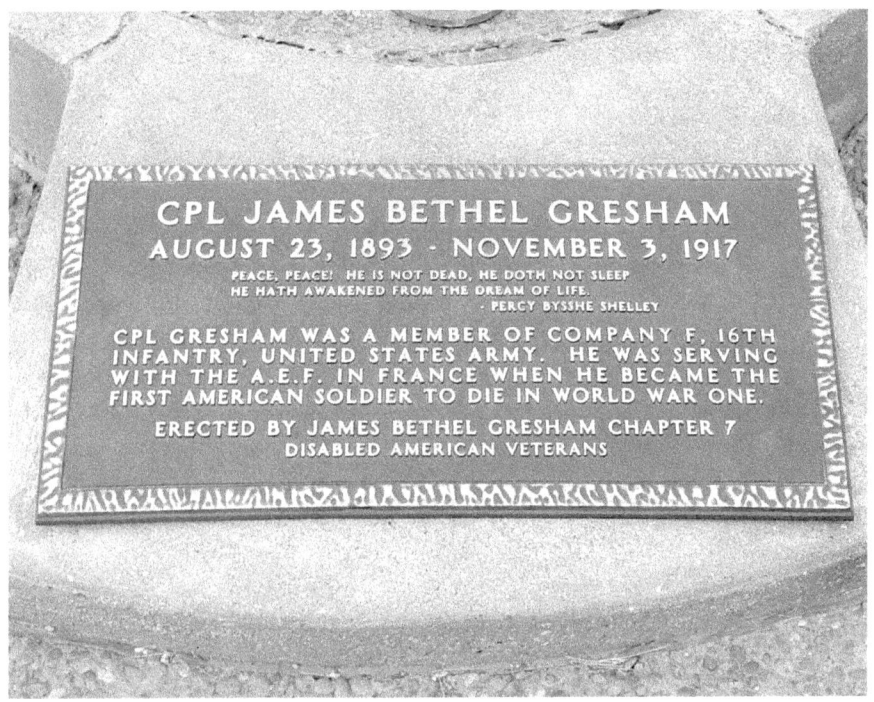

Gresham memorial plaque at flagpole base. *Courtesy of the author.*

The James Bethel Gresham Chapter 7 of the Disabled American Veterans sponsored the plaque for Gresham in the old military plot at Evansville's Locust Hill Cemetery. The small metal rectangle is cemented to the base of a flagpole. Atop the tall shaft, Old Glory flutters above the military-style tombstones of Gresham and several other soldiers from World Wars I and II, the Spanish-American War and the Civil War.

"CPL GRESHAM WAS A MEMBER OF COMPANY F, 16TH INFANTRY, UNITED STATES ARMY," the tablet tells cemetery visitors. "HE WAS SERVING WITH THE A.E.F. IN FRANCE WHEN HE BECAME THE FIRST AMERICAN SOLDIER TO DIE IN WORLD WAR ONE."

Gresham's grave marker is in the front ranks of the simple white marble tombstones that stand soldierlike on a grassy hilltop in the cemetery. Born in Beech Grove, near Calhoun, on August 23, 1893, Gresham moved with his family to Evansville in 1901.

"He was an ordinary American, with no distinction of high birth, scholarship, or social prestige," Heiman Blatt wrote in *Sons of Men: Evansville's War Record*, published in 1920. "As a typical American he did not bully or bluster but only went to defend and vindicate a cause which is national in its inherency and universal in its application."

Gresham joined the army in 1914 and served in Texas on the Mexican border. He earned corporal's stripes and shipped out to France in 1917.

Just before sunup on November 3, 1917, Gresham and two other American soldiers, Privates Thomas Enright and Merle Hay, were killed when the Germans raided their trench in Bathelemont, France, according to *The United States in the World War* by John B. McMaster. Markers at Beech Grove and at the Gresham Bridge say Gresham was the first to fall. An enemy soldier shot him between the eyes, the *Evansville Courier* newspaper reported in 1966.

German artillery cut off Gresham and his buddies from the rest of their outfit. The doomed men "fought gallantly until overwhelmed solely by numbers," the *Courier* said on November 6, 1917. The story—an Associated Press dispatch—said that "the fighting…was hand to hand. It was brief and fierce in the extreme."

Gresham and the other slain doughboys were buried on the slope of a nearby hill. "The site a few months later was marked by a stone monument bearing the name and regiment of each of the dead, and the inscription: 'Here lie the first soldiers of the great Republic of the United States who died on the soil of France for justice and liberty, November 3, 1917,'" McMaster wrote.

General Bordeaux, the French commander of the sector where Gresham, Enright and Hay died, took charge of the burial in what became the American Cemetery at Bathelemont-les-Bauzemont, according to the *Owensboro Messenger-Inquirer* newspaper. The general, his staff and a representative of the French Corps commander watched "as the bodies of these first heroes were lowered in the grave" while "a company of United States soldiers fired three volleys, and the trumpeter sounded taps," according to *Indiana World War Records, Gold Star Honor Roll*.

The book also says that Bordeaux gave a speech bidding farewell to Gresham, Enright and Hay "in the name of the French Army, and in the name of France."

The general added:

> *Of their own free will they had left their happy and prosperous country to come over here. They knew that the war continues in Europe; they knew that the forces fighting for honor, love, justice, civilization, were still checked by the long-prepared forces which are serving the powers of brutal domination, oppression, barbarity. They knew that an effort was still necessary.*

World War I

Bordeaux predicted that

> *their families, their friends, and their fellow-citizens will be proud when they learn of their death…These graves, the first to be dug in our national soil, at but a short distance from the enemy, are as a mark of the mighty hand of our allies, firmly clinging to the common task, confirming the will of the people and Army of the United States to fight with us to a finish; ready to sacrifice as long as it will be necessary, until final victory for the noblest of causes—that of liberty of nations, the weak as well as the mighty.*

Bordeaux asked

> *that the mortal remains of these young men be left here—be left to us forever…The passer-by will stop and uncover his head. The travelers of France, of the allied countries, of America, the men of heart who will come to visit our battlefield of Lorraine, will go out of their way to come here,—to bring to these graves the tribute of their respect and of their gratefulness.*

Despite Bordeaux's plea, the bodies of Gresham, Enright and Hay were sent home and reburied in American soil. In July 1921, Pershing traveled to Hoboken, New Jersey, to meet two transport ships carrying the remains of Gresham, Enright, Hay and more than seven thousand other U.S. soldiers killed in France.

The coffins were gently lined up on the pier; an American flag draped each one. Pershing laid a wreath on the coffins of Gresham, Enright and Hay.

"These men who died on foreign soil laid down their lives for us," Pershing said. "They fought for freedom and for eternal right and justice, as did the founders of the great American Republic before them."

A military band played "Onward Christian Soldiers" and "The Star-Spangled Banner." A solitary bugler sounded "Taps."

A train took Gresham home to Indiana. On July 12–13, the corporal's body lay in state at the Indiana capitol in Indianapolis, where a memorial service was held for him, wrote A.A. Hoehling in his book, *The Fierce Lambs*.

Gresham's body arrived at the Evansville train station on July 14, after which he lay in state at Veterans' Memorial Coliseum. Mourners were led by the soldier's mother, Alice Gresham Dodd.

Gresham's father, a Civil War veteran, died when James was seven. Alice Gresham married Bill Dodd. The union was not prosperous, the *Courier* said.

Alice wanted a private service at the family's modest home before the public rites, according to the *Courier*. "Funeral home workers couldn't get [Gresham's] casket through the front door," the newspaper explained. "A wall in the entry was too close to the door; the casket had to be hoisted through a large window."

Townsfolk raised money to build a new house for Alice Dodd, who lived in it until she died in 1928, according to the Evansville newspaper. The city owns the small dwelling, which is unoccupied.

Gresham was buried in Locust Hill Cemetery on July 16 following funeral services at Simpson Memorial Methodist Episcopal Church, Hoehling added. More tragedy followed for Alice Gresham Dodd, the *Courier* reported. She had to bury two more of her children in 1918—local victims of a worldwide influenza epidemic that killed millions.

James Bethel Gresham "did not claim descent from Mayflower stock; he held no college degree; and he was not enrolled among our mercantile aristocracy and captains of industry," Blatt wrote. "Only an average American; yet, his name will be transmitted to posterity as the first American soldier who made the supreme sacrifice on the battlefield."

"Funny How They Treat Some Div."

Penciled inside the front cover of Private First Class Robert McCune's World War I diary is a request: "Notice—If I am shot will the person who finds this book please send it to the address on the next page. Thank you."

The handwriting is hard to make out, but not so much because time has dimmed the words. The message is punctured; a faded brown stain covers most of it. The stain is Robert McCune's blood.

The German bullet that killed him made the hole. McCune, a twenty-two-year-old Paducahan, fell near Soissons, France, on July 18, 1918. He was trying to save a wounded officer, "presenting himself as a target to a German sharpshooter," reads one of McCune's posthumous citations for bravery. Pershing and another general signed it.

As McCune wished, the diary got home to 1015 Trimble Street, the address of his grandmother, Sarah McCune. He was staying with her when he joined the army.

Generations of McCunes have treasured the four- by six-inch leather-bound diary. Cathy and Mike McCune of Lone Oak have it now. Mike is Robert McCune's second cousin. The McCunes also have the soldier's bullet-shattered gold pocket watch.

"We are very proud to have such an amazing piece of history," Cathy McCune said. "It especially means a lot to me to because he started it the day he enlisted, and it was with him the day he died."

World War I

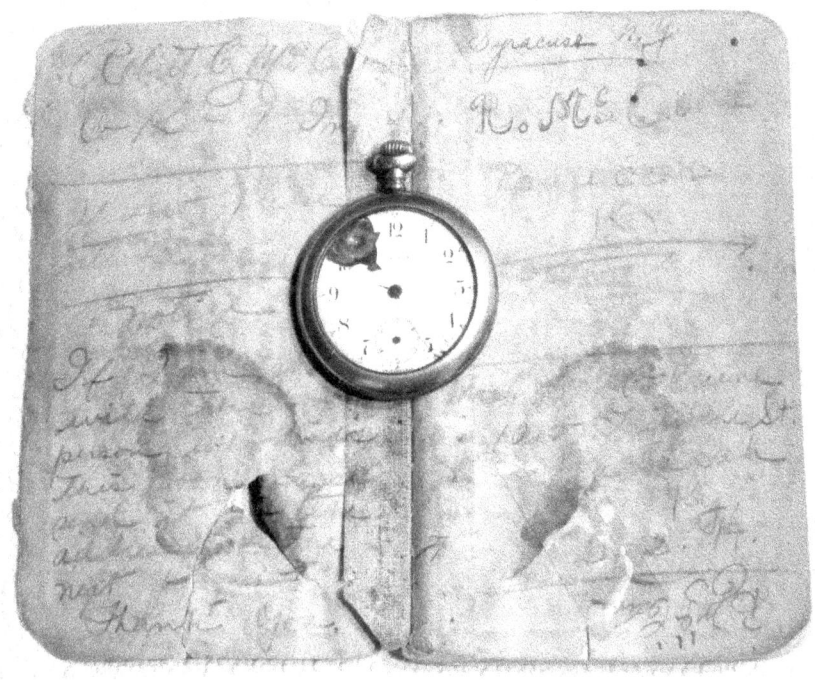

McCune's diary and pocket watch. *Courtesy of the author.*

The army first buried McCune in a military cemetery near Soissons. After the war, the army returned his body to Paducah for reburial in Oak Grove Cemetery. The McCunes also have photos of the soldier, his grave in France and a file of newspaper clippings about his death, burial and the diary. "Probably no funeral in the city's history has been more largely attended," the *Paducah Evening Sun* reported.

The diary is a remarkably detailed record of military life in World War I from the citizen-soldier's perspective. It starts on July 2, 1917, the day McCune volunteered for the army in Paducah. It ends on July 10, 1918, eight days before he died.

McCune left his hometown by train, arriving at Fort Thomas, Kentucky, to start basic training. It was the Fourth of July.

McCune wrote that his army uniform fit pretty well. But "some of the boys sure did look funny, their uniforms were a mile to [*sic*] large or small for them…about half had to exchange."

On July 17, the army ordered McCune to a camp at Syracuse, New York. "Nobody felt sorry as we were getting very tired of…[Fort Thomas]." His troop train crept through Cincinnati "at a mile a week…the boys are yelling like a picnic, everybody waving at us, some waving flags."

McCune found Syracuse "not near as good as Ft. Thomas." He filled his diary with dreary accounts of long marches, close-order drill and the other universal soldier gripe: kitchen police. McCune pulled what the army called "kitchen police," or "k.p," duty on August 19. It was a Sunday, the only free day he had. "Some job never stopped all day, never peeled so many spuds in all my life."

The army put McCune in the Ninth Infantry Regiment. On September 18, 1917—"the greatest of all" days, according to McCune's diary—the Ninth Infantry went overseas. The doughboys boarded a British troopship at Hoboken, New Jersey, and "sailed for some where unknown," McCune wrote. The destination was Liverpool, England, via Halifax, Nova Scotia.

It was no pleasure cruise, McCune wrote. He disdained the ship, RMS *Carmania*, as "an old tub." He disparaged the crew as "crazy" English, "little runts and funny looking people…If they could fight half as good, as they talk tough, we would not have to help them, all they can say is 'bloomin bloody.'"

Seasickness plagued the regiment, including McCune. "Anything you do, you can't get rid of it, when you see or think about anything to eat, you nearly die." For troops feeling well enough to eat, food was "junk" that "would kill an army mule," according to McCune.

The real death threat was unseen: German submarines. Soldiers had to help sailors stand watch for U-boats, which prowled far into the Atlantic. "Every precaution is taken, wearing life belts all the time and have orders to sleep with our clothes on, a guard of five hundred men are on, half on each side of ship," McCune wrote.

Near the English coast, the *Carmania* rendezvoused with a dozen small Royal Navy submarine chasers. McCune was glad to see them. "They sure are fast. Feel like sleeping tonight," he wrote.

The troopship safely docked at Liverpool on October 2. The Ninth herded onto a troop train bound for the English Channel port of Southampton. Beyond lay France and the bloody Western Front.

On October 5, a side-wheel steamer ferried the Ninth Infantry to Le Havre. Another train deposited the doughboys at Beaumont. After a foot trek of twelve miles—"meanest hike I ever knew as we had nothing to eat for twenty four hours," McCune wrote—the regiment pitched its tents at Soulacourt. Somebody told McCune that only a dozen miles separated the regiment from the battlefront.

World War I

McCune, now a private first class, filled his diary with gripes about rain, cold, fatigue, food shortages and delayed visits from the paymaster. "If I ever get out of this army they will never get me again…Nearly dead now so tired, have had wet feet since I have been here. They are getting soft from being wet and drilling so much. The worst part of it is, we do not get half enough to eat, would give my salary for a square meal."

It snowed in late October. But McCune wrote that even though "nearly every one is starved around there, there is not one who is afraid to fight and die for the dear old U.S. even if she does not feed us good."

McCune never used "dear old" to describe France and the French:

> *Our feet are nearly rottened* [sic] *off, been wet ever since we have been in France. This is the damnest* [sic] *country in the world, if they would give it to the Germans they would give it back gladly. These F'men sure love U.S. soldiers. They only charge us four or five times higher than they do the natives. If you have a five franc bill you have to spend it all, they will not give any silver for change. The sun even has no use for this part of the country. It never shines here, rain and cold weather all the time.*

The army fed the regiment a hot turkey dinner for Thanksgiving. But McCune had a cold and didn't enjoy the holiday meal. "Aching, and paining all over," he wrote.

McCune was feeling better by December 6 when he "recived [sic] a nice box of cakes and candy from Miss Kreutzer, sure fine, and makes a person feel like one is not forgotten at home." Apparently Myra Kreutzer sent the sweets. He put her name and Trimble Street address in the diary. There are other names from back home: Louise Beeler, Winnie Bazzel, Marguerette McCune (his half sister) and W.H. Morrison.

Also on December 6, McCune wrote that he was now a scout in the automatic rifle squad. "Nice job, all you have to do is go ahead of all, and then you do not have to worry how to get back as the German sharpshooters take care of that for you. But I think I will try it once."

Christmas 1917—his last—was joyless. McCune spent the day "hard at work…Pick and shovel all the time. The ground frozen about ten inches."

One can only guess about the rest of the winter of 1917–1918. McCune didn't write anything in his diary from December 25 to March 18, 1918. Then, he predicted "bigger…[things] are to take place."

Some time before, McCune's outfit had edged closer to the fighting. He was just four miles behind the trenches. He watched French and German warplanes dogfight in the sky overhead. "The French planes protect us all they can, but the botches [evidently McCune's version of "Boche," the French epithet for Germans] are determined to find us, a number of them have fell and only one French plane that we know of."

Finally, he made it to the front lines. On April 7, McCune wrote that he had spent "a few days in the trenches…Seen very little but have plenty of big shells busting around us all the time, up to-date only a few of our men are wounded."

He didn't write again until May 19. By then, he had "put in two hitches in the trenches, had a hell of a time." His next entry was on June 1: "Arrived at Hill 201—just a little northwest of Chateau Tierry [*sic*]."

The Germans had begun their last great win-the-war offensive on the Western Front. The Ninth Infantry was helping hold the Allied line in the Bellau Wood/Chateau Thierry sector. McCune continued:

> *Very much shelling, but they don't seem to do much damage, have lost about 40 of our men Lt. Logil killed while going across an open place. He was the best Lt. I ever saw, had a long talk with him a few hours before it happened, and his platoon sure show that they miss him, he was the quietest and would never duck from a shell, at present I have his cane, also his belt and pistol case.*

The Allies stopped the German drive; casualties were heavy on both sides. In all of June, the U.S. Second Army Division—of which the Ninth Regiment was a part—lost 9,777 men killed or wounded. McCune figured they had earned a rest.

On July 10, McCune was angry. He heard there would be no respite for the bloodied Ninth Infantry. "Funny how they treat some div. After 41 days on the front line we are now relieved to back up the French." He wrote no more in his diary.

A rainstorm drenched the battlefield around Soissons on the morning of July 18, 1918, according to historian S.L.A. Marshall. The Second Division was up early. By 7:00 a.m., the doughboys had pushed out of Soissons, grabbed high ground around Vierzy and shoved the Germans out of Vierzy Ravine. Having stopped the Germans, the Allies were now attacking to win the war.

Desperately, the Germans fought back. Some time on July 18, enemy fire struck Lieutenant Colonel Alfred C. Arnold, McCune's battalion commander. The officer went down in a clearing wide open to enemy fire.

McCune ran toward the wounded officer. A German soldier fired. The bullet struck McCune in the chest, ripping through uniform, diary, flesh and bone. He fell.

World War I

The army said Private First Class Robert C. McCune, Company L, First Battalion, Ninth Infantry Regiment, Second Division, "died with honor in the service of his country." The army also said he died quickly, the fatal bullet piercing his heart.

Apparently, a second bullet hit McCune. His gold Locust pocket watch stopped that round, which shattered the crystal and tore off the hands. It pinged the watch face between the numbers ten and eleven.

McCune couldn't have known it. But he died on the day that led to what Marshall called "the great retreat of the Germans."

Writing in *The American Heritage History of World War I*, he explained:

> *There would be no more furious* [German General Erich] *Ludendorff lunges, no carving of great sailents. The forward march initiated by* [French general and supreme Allied commander Ferdinand] *Foch would keep going. Great anticlimactic battles were still to be fought. At least a million men had to die or bleed to prove that point. But the decision came on July 18 when the last straw broke the Teuton back.*

The army buried McCune in a military cemetery at Ploisy, France, near where he died. A simple white wooden cross giving his name, rank and outfit marked the grave, no. 192.

The diary got home. An American lieutenant found it; a French general forwarded it to Sarah McCune.

Almost three years after the war was over, McCune was back home. Ex-doughboys of American Legion Post 31 saw to the reburial of McCune's body in Oak Grove Cemetery. It was the Paducah post's first military funeral.

On May 15, 1921, the *Sun* reported, "the body of the young soldier was laid to rest under stately oaks, fragrant spring flowers banking the grave." A special squad of city police handled traffic; one thousand cars were parked in the cemetery, the *Sun* added.

Dr. John L. Weber, Legion Post 31 chaplain, officiated at services in Roth Undertaking Chapel. A caisson and limber bore McCune's flag-draped coffin to the cemetery.

The International Order of Oddfellows Band provided funeral music. Legionnaires fired a salute as McCune's body was lowered into the grave.

A gray stone slab covers McCune's grave. It says J.B. and Maggie McCune's son died at Chateau-Thierry, the name of the big battle area that included Soissons. Near the foot of the stone is a soldier's simple epitaph: "He willingly gave his life for his country."

"With His Own Hands He Pinned This Badge of Glory"

Sergeant John William Kevil came home to Paducah wearing a French field marshal's medal on his uniform.

Soldiers like the young western Kentuckian proved "that the color of a man's skin had nothing to do with the color of a man's soul," wrote a famous war correspondent from Kevil's hometown. His name was Irvin S. Cobb.

Kevil, the descendant of slaves, earned high praise and a medal for bravery from one of France's top generals. The Paducahan wore sergeant's stripes in the 814th Pioneer Infantry, an African American outfit commanded by white officers. Joseph Joffre, marshal of France, gave Kevil his own Croix de Guerre.

Joffre took it off his uniform and pinned it on Kevil. Looking on were Pershing and a British marshal, Sir Douglas Haig, according to Cobb, who witnessed the ceremony.

John William Kevil. *Courtesy of the McCracken County Public Library.*

World War I

Racism tinged most stories white U.S. war correspondents wrote about black troops. By today's standards, Cobb's writing was patronizing and stereotyped blacks.

But Cobb's biographer said that he rebuked the deep-seated racial prejudice of his era. While Cobb used "dialect humor," he seldom made African American soldiers the butt of jokes like other reporters did, said Anita Lawson, a former Murray State University English professor and author of *Irvin S. Cobb*.

More often, he "was impressed with their bravery and discipline, and described their behavior fired by the perspective of a Southern background," Lawson wrote in her book, the first scholarly biography of Cobb, a journalist, fiction writer and humorist who was born in Paducah in 1876.

Cobb covered World War I for the *Saturday Evening Post* magazine. Lawson said several African American newspapers reprinted Cobb's articles. "Cobb discovered to his amazement that he had become a hero to blacks all over the country," Lawson wrote.

She also said Cobb paid tribute to Kevil during the 1918 Christmas holidays in Paducah. "Practically the entire black population of the town" escorted Cobb to Washington Street Baptist Church where he delivered a powerful oration in honor of Kevil, who was still overseas, Lawson wrote.

In *Exit Laughing*, published in 1941, Cobb wrote that the Yule program was his "greatest thrill."

The *Honor Roll of McCracken County*, a 1919 book with pictures and brief biographies of local World War I veterans, said Kevil was born on February 6, 1891. His parents were Silas and Della Kevil.

In *Exit Laughing*, Cobb wrote that, in his speech at the church, he withheld Kevil's name for dramatic effect, explaining to the crowd that he was visiting the soldier's colonel in France when word came that "a certain non-commissioned officer" from Paducah wanted to see him. Cobb praised Kevil "for leading a successful attack on a German machine-gun nest and taking, almost single-handedly, that machine gun's crew."

But Cobb seemed most eloquent when he described the event in which his fellow Paducahan received one of France's highest military honors:

> *On that sunny afternoon, with the distant roar of the cannons in their ears, the picked forces of three great allied armies of three great nations formed three sides of a great hollow square.*
>
> *Over here showed the horizon blue of veteran French poilus* [soldiers]. *Across there were the hard-fighting British. And yonder at the top of the square, lined up khaki-clad the ranks of the Yanks.*

At the opening of the bottom of the pocket, near where I was, were three older men abreast. And one of these men was General Sir Douglas Haig, Field Marshal of Great Britain, and another was the beloved "Papa" Joffre, Generalissimo of France, and the third was John J. Pershing, Commander in Chief of the American Expeditionary Force.

And then a command rang out like a bugle, and with a mighty rattle of weapons, all these soldiers came to salute and the trooped colors of twenty regiments blared forth in the strains of the Marseillais Hymn [the French national anthem].

And on that, from the front row of the Americans, there stepped forth the erect figure of one Negro soldier. He marched the length of that oblong until he came to a halt and stood at attention facing those three great commanders.

The white-haired Papa Joffre took from among the glittering array of decorations on his own breast the scrap of metal alloy with its adornment of red and green ribbon—the tiny emblem which, whenever fighting men get together, stands for gallantry in the highest; and with his own hands he pinned this badge of glory on the breast of that lone soldier and kissed him upon both his cheeks.

Finally, Cobb said, he named Kevil—though he misspelled the name as "Kivil" in *Exit Laughing*. The crowd cheered and applauded, he added.

The *Honor Roll*—which segregated African American vets at the back of the book—said Kevil joined the army on July 16, 1918, and "served five months in the U.S. and two months overseas."

Kevil survived the war and came home to a Jim Crow Paducah. Segregation and race discrimination would remain the law and the social order until well beyond World War II.

In her book, Lawson quoted Cobb, who said that "the color of a man's skin hasn't anything to do with the color of his soul." Few white Americans agreed when World War I ended in 1918. "Back in America, Negro veterans were subjected to the same discriminations that plagued them before and during the war," wrote Francis Butler Simkins and Charles P. Roland in *A History of the South*. "World War I resulted in greater freedom for Poles, Yugoslavs, and Czechoslovaks, but not for the American Negro."

Kevil returned to Paducah, but he later moved to Chicago, where he became an undertaker, according to Paul Kevil, his nephew. Kevil died on February 19, 1947. He was buried in what was then the African American part of Oak Grove Cemetery. Cobb, who died in 1944, was buried in what was the white section of the old burial ground.

World War I

Meanwhile, Cobb championed the cause of other African American veterans. "He spoke at Carnegie Hall with Theodore Roosevelt in support of relief for black soldiers," Lawson wrote in *The Kentucky Encyclopedia*.

Madisonville Man Named the American Legion

When American soldiers met in Paris, France, after World War I to found "the world's greatest veterans' organization," they couldn't decide what to call it.

Somebody proposed Liberty League. Somebody else liked American Crusaders. American Legion of the Great War was suggested, too.

But in the end, Major Maurice K. Gordon of Madisonville provided the name that stuck. He suggested American Legion.

According to an old Madisonville newspaper story, "Historians…accord Major Gordon the honor of naming the American Legion at Paris, France, March 15 to 17, 1919, at which the world's greatest veterans' organization was born." In his book, *A History of the American Legion*, Richard Seeyle Jones wrote that Gordon "moved to adopt" the name American Legion after debate was "waged with vigor."

Gordon practiced law in Madisonville, the Hopkins County seat, for more than sixty-five years. He died in 1974 at age ninety-six.

Gordon was inspector general of the Thirty-sixth Division in World War I. The western Kentuckian was among one thousand officers and men who gathered in the old Cirque de Paris opera house and started the American Legion.

Gordon arrived in the French capital aboard a machine gun truck. "There was a general chat about the big caucus soon to meet," Gordon told his hometown paper. "Someone asked what the organization would be called. I was one of those who tried to answer every question, so I said, 'The American Legion.'

"This was pure inspiration. We all knew of the French Foreign Legion, of the Roman Legions…The Legion of Honor and the Loyal Legion also came to mind. The boys liked the suggestion."

But at the convention, a majority of the Committee on Name proposed Legion of the Great War. Veterans of the Great War was the panel's second choice, according to *A History of the American Legion*. When Gordon rose to propose the American Legion another delegate wanted "of the Great War," Jones also wrote.

Gordon told the Madisonville paper that the Committee on Name reported several more submissions for names.

> *They included Liberty League, American Crusaders, Legion of the Great War and Comrades in Service. The name American Legion of the Great War was favored by some as the initial letters "ALGW" were supposed to suggest Abraham Lincoln and George Washington.*
>
> *Debate on the various names ensued at length. The debate seemed to be uninteresting. So when I could get to the floor I moved the adoption of the name "The American Legion." There was objection that it had a silk stocking sound. The caucus did not consider that objection seriously and with practical unanimity adopted the name.*

In 1960, the national Legion organization awarded Gordon a citation which said that "the name 'American Legion,' conceived by Major Maurice K. Gordon…has become a household word synonymous with patriotism and Americanism." In 1969, in honor of the American Legion's fiftieth birthday, the Kentucky branch gave Gordon a silver medallion.

In 1975, Madisonville Legion Post 6 was named the Maurice K. Gordon American Legion Post 6.

CHAPTER 7

WORLD WAR II

"IF WE HADN'T BEEN UP IN THE MAINMAST, WE WOULDN'T HAVE MADE IT"

December 7, 1941, seemed like an ordinary Sunday morning in port for Gunner's Mate Third Class James Allard Vessels of Paducah.

His ship, the USS *Arizona*, was one of seven battlewagons moored in Pearl Harbor, Hawaii. The navy called the lineup of powerful dreadnoughts Battleship Row.

Vessels rolled out of his bunk about five-thirty in the morning. He pulled on his uniform, ate breakfast and headed topside for a friendly game of acey-deucy on the antiaircraft deck.

He never finished the card game. At 7:55 a.m., Japanese warplanes attacked, bombing America into World War II.

The 608-foot *Arizona*, BB 39, was a prime target. "When general quarters sounded, I ran for my battle station up in the mainmast," said Vessels, then twenty years old.

He and eight shipmates climbed to an antiaircraft machine gun nest atop the three-legged steel tower.

"When we got there, we found out that the four fifty-caliber machine guns didn't have any ammunition," he said. "But before anybody could go below for ammunition, the ship blew up."

James Vessels. *Courtesy of the Market House Museum, Paducah.*

A Japanese bomb sank the 31,400-ton dreadnought. "The concussion tore most of our clothes off," Vessels said. "But if we hadn't been up in the mainmast, we wouldn't have made it."

From their lofty vantage point, Vessels and the other sailors watched helplessly as the Japanese aviators bombed, torpedoed and strafed the U.S. fleet. "The Japanese torpedo bombers came in barely above naval housing on the main island and would have to bank sharply to avoid hitting the *Arizona*," he said.

"They came so close we could see the pilots thumb their noses at us. The rear gunners tried to machine gun us, but they couldn't get their guns lowered enough and the bullets whizzed over our heads."

After the fires on the *Arizona* subsided, Vessels and the others came down from the mainmast. They were horrified by what they saw.

The forward part of their ship, blackened by fire and shrouded in choking, dark smoke, was a heap of twisted and broken steel. Vessels saw a dead officer on the searchlight deck—about halfway down the mainmast. The heat from the fires had curled back the soles of his shoes.

On the antiaircraft deck, he saw just one man standing, a sailor named Collins. He was so badly burned that Vessels recognized him only because he was tall.

Casualties on the *Arizona* included 1,117 dead out of a crew of 1,448, according to the National Park Service. Almost half of those killed in the attack were sailors and marines on the *Arizona*, according to *Day of Infamy* by Walter Lord.

Besides the *Arizona*, seventeen ships were sunk or seriously damaged, and 188 planes were destroyed at their bases around Pearl Harbor and elsewhere on the island of Oahu, Lord added.

"That night we expected an attack by the Japanese army," Vessels said. 'We were prepared to go into the hills and fight it out if we had to."

The attack did not come. The Japanese fleet, including the six aircraft carriers from which the enemy planes had taken off, was steaming away.

Vessels spent most of World War II in Pearl Harbor doing salvage work and helping man an honor guard that buried sailors and marines killed in faraway island battles with names like Guadalcanal, Tarawa, Saipan, Iwo Jima and Okinawa.

He said he did not hate the Japanese for almost killing him on December 7, 1941. "I guess they were just following orders the same as we would have followed orders from our commander in chief."

In 1971, Vessels, who was a member of the Pearl Harbor Survivors Association, returned to Hawaii and visited the gleaming white memorial that straddles the hull of the old ship, the outline of which is visible just below the water.

On one wall of the structure is a roll of the *Arizona*'s crew who died in the attack. The names include Gunner's Mate Third Class Worth Ross Lightfoot, Vessel's partner at acey-deucy.

THE SAILOR WHO READ HIS OWN OBITUARY

The navy gave Jim Hamlin up for dead on December 7, 1941.

A sailor aboard the battleship USS *California*, BB 44, Hamlin was listed as killed in the Pearl Harbor attack. His parents in Harlan, Kentucky, were grief stricken when they learned of their son's death in a telegram dated December 16, 1941.

"The Navy Department deeply regrets to inform you that your son, James Thomas Hamlin, fireman first class, U.S. Navy, was lost in action in the performance of his duty and in the service of his country," the wire read.

Special services in Hamlin's honor were held at his church, Harlan Baptist. Hamlin's obituary ran in the *Harlan Enterprise*, where he had been a cub sports reporter.

His death notice was premature. Hamlin survived the Pearl Harbor attacks and the rest of World War II. He died in 1999.

Hamlin settled in Lone Oak, his wife's hometown, after the war. He treasured the telegram and another one, dated December 31, the navy sent apologizing for the mistake. "How many people do you know who can say they've read their own obituary?" he asked.

December 7, 1941, began promisingly enough for Hamlin, twenty-nine, whose 624-foot ship was nicknamed the Prune Barge for the seemingly endless supply of that dried fruit the crew received from the state of California.

Like Saturday, December 6, Sunday, December 7, was another duty-free day for Hamlin, "liberty" in navy lingo. He was looking forward to swimming and sunbathing with some of his shipmates at Waikiki Beach, which he had visited the day before.

He also had stopped by the Honolulu Montgomery Ward store and bought a $9.95 radio for his steady girl back in Lone Oak, a Paducah suburb. The clerk promised the sailor the radio would be shipped promptly to Almyra Craig, whom he had met in Lone Oak in 1937. They were married in 1943.

After pulling on his uniform of white shorts and white jumper, Hamlin went to breakfast. Having eaten, he went topside and got a copy of the *Honolulu Advertiser* from "Sweatshirt" Clark, the *California*'s unofficial paperboy when the battlewagon was in port, Hamlin said.

Hamlin found a shady spot forward under a big canvas awning that had been spread for church services below the ship's number one fourteen-inch gun turret. But the breeze made it hard for Hamlin to turn the pages of his paper, so he went below.

At 7:55 a.m., an air-raid alarm sounded on the battleship. "I thought it was a heck of a time to have an air-raid drill," he said. "But it didn't take me long to realize it wasn't a drill."

Japanese aerial torpedoes tore gaping holes in the *California*, the flagship of the Pacific battleship fleet. "The torpedoes shook the ship," he said. "Dust started falling off overhead and we thought we were being gassed."

Hamilton and six men went for gas masks. A chief petty officer stopped them and ordered Hamlin to Number Three Fire Room to help get the ship underway.

World War II

Minutes later, a bomb crashed into the *California* and exploded where the masks were stored. "I don't know whether or not those men were killed, but I never saw them again," Hamlin said.

By the time he joined other sailors in the fire room, bombs and torpedoes had crippled the battleship. The *California* was going nowhere, except to the shallow bottom of Pearl Harbor.

When the abandon ship order was given, Hamlin found his way off the ship blocked by fire and debris.

Seeking another escape route, he saw a sailor slumped against a bulkhead. He recognized the man as one of the clerks in the *California*'s "geedunk" stand, where cigarettes, ice cream and candy were sold. "We laid him on a couch in the ward room," Hamlin said. "We found out later he was dead."

When Hamlin reached the main deck, he caught a glimpse of what he thought "was the biggest submarine I'd ever seen." It was the USS *Oklahoma*'s 583-foot hull. Torpedoes had plowed into the warship, causing it to capsize. The navy said 429 of its crew perished.

Before he leaped into the water, he saw musical instruments scattered over the *California*'s main deck. "One of the men in the band later told me they had just started to play the National Anthem when the Japanese planes started coming in. He said they never played faster in their lives and finished."

Hamlin swam for a nearby lifeboat, arriving just as a Japanese plane strafed it. "That boat was just too slow for me," he said. "I swam the rest of the way to Ford Island."

Hamlin found refuge in an airplane hangar that was crowded with sailors, soldiers, marines and airmen. "It seemed to dawn on everybody at the same time that this was a fine target, and we all scattered," Hamlin said.

He spent the rest of the attack in a nearby ditch.

After the Japanese planes flew back to their aircraft carriers, Hamlin and other sailors returned to the *California* to fight fires and try to keep it afloat. Their efforts were to no avail; the ship sank, its main deck and superstructure still above water.

Hamlin and the others worked almost until midnight salvaging equipment and gear off the *California*. Bone tired, he narrowly escaped death again when he fell off a gangway into the dark water. An officer ordered him to go ashore and get some sleep.

"He told me that wherever I went to go whistling or singing because they were shooting anything that moved," Hamlin said. "I don't remember what I sang, but I remember I said, 'Please don't shoot me' at the end of every verse."

Hamlin bedded down in the balcony of Ford Island Theater. Not until morning did he notice that his white uniform had been ruined. Japanese torpedoes ripped open the *California*'s fuel oil bunkers. Hamlin swam through the oil slick to Ford Island.

He rummaged through a big pile of clothes collected from all over and made himself a new uniform. It was not exactly regulation: navy chambray work shirt, khaki trousers, a brown marine shoe and a black navy shoe.

He was wearing that unlikely getup when he joined the crew of the USS *Chicago*, a heavy cruiser that steamed into Pearl Harbor after the attack and then left to fight the Japanese. Because he was gone, navy authorities at Pearl Harbor presumably believed he had gone down with the *California*.

He was on the *Chicago* in 1942 for the Battles of the Coral Sea and Guadalcanal. He emerged unhurt again when an enemy torpedo damaged the cruiser's bow off Savo Island, near Guadalcanal, on August 9. Hamlin escaped death once more when Japanese warplanes damaged and sank the *Chicago* on January 29–30, 1943.

He was serving on the USS *LaSalle*, a transport ship, when it landed marines at the Battle of Tarawa in November 1943. "I remember singing 'I'll be home for Christmas' when we put them ashore at Tarawa," Hamlin said. "A lot of them didn't make it, though."

In June 1944, the *LaSalle* landed troops at Saipan. The *California*, refloated and repaired, helped bombard the Japanese fortifications.

It was the first time he had seen his old ship since the Pearl Harbor attack. "Go get 'em, Prune Barge!" Hamlin hollered through his tears.

After earning five battle stars in the Pacific Theater, he was shipped stateside in 1944. He was a master-at-arms at Navy Shore Patrol headquarters in Chicago when the war in the Pacific ended on September 2, 1945.

Hamlin left the navy in 1946. Almyra preceded him in death in 1997.

Hamlin said he did not hate the Japanese, though they sank two ships from under him. "They were just following orders like we were," he said. "I don't hate them, and I hope they don't hate me either."

"I Took My First Paycheck and Made a Down Payment on a Fur Coat"

Margaret Carrico "always thought of those navy boys" every time she approved a shipment of 20 mm cannon shells from the Viola ammunition plant.

World War II

"I didn't want a shell of mine to explode in a gun and hurt somebody or not go off when they shot it. If a shell wasn't right, I sent it back."

Carrico spent much of World War II inspecting ammunition at the big National Fireworks Factory near Viola in Graves County. The facility was one of only six plants in the United States that turned out 20 mm shells for small, rapid-firing antiaircraft guns mounted on U.S. warships.

There is no way to know for sure. But Carrico figured Viola-made shells brought down or damaged their share of Japanese warplanes. "Most of the shells made were shipped to the Pacific," said C.T. Winslow, a navy inspector at the plant, about a dozen miles north of Mayfield.

The Viola ordnance works sprouted on 1,500 acres of rich farmland. It grew into one of the largest defense plants in Kentucky.

There is nothing to commemorate the factory except the memories of plant workers; most have died. "Around here, it was the place to work," said Rosalyn Gibson, another inspector. "Oh, my, the money was good. I took my first paycheck and made a down payment on a fur coat."

Only a few of the plant's two dozen or so main buildings survive. They are strange-looking concrete structures that tell no tales of war. The plant site has been divided by barbed wire fences and conquered by soybean and corn patches.

Operated by the National Fireworks Company of West Hanover, Massachusetts, the plant opened on September 19, 1942. Senate majority leader Alben Barkley, a Paducah Democrat, and Representative Noble J. Gregory, a Mayfield Democrat, were "tireless in their efforts to bring the plant to this community," the *Mayfield Messenger* reported.

The navy said plant employees, members of Chemical Workers Union Local 151, worked tirelessly, too. The factory won a coveted army-navy "E" pennant for excellence in war production.

Plant workers also were generous with their pay. They bought $1 million worth of war bonds and earned the right to also run a special "Minute Man T" banner up the flagpole.

"We all felt a lot of patriotism working out there," said Frances Wilson, a secretary. "A lot of the women had husbands or sweethearts in the service. There were also older men who couldn't go, and they felt like they were doing their part."

Carrico worked where high-explosive gunpowder was mixed. "They wouldn't even let women comb their hair because of the static electricity and the risk of an explosion," she said. "That powder was hard on you, too. It made your hair and your hands turn yellow. A lot of people were scared to work in there, but I didn't mind."

The ordnance works, which closed in 1945—the last year of the war—covered more ground than the town of Viola did. The plant workforce of close to three thousand was probably ten times larger than the entire population of Viola and nearby West Viola.

"It Was Another Step on the Road"

Anna Mac Clarke of Anderson County answered Mary McLeod Bethune's call for "one black WAAC."

"Bethune delivered the commencement address to the Kentucky State College class of 1941, which included Clarke," said Trowbridge. "Clarke enlisted in the newly formed Women's Army Auxiliary Corps on October 3, 1942, at Cincinnati."

Haley Bowling as Clarke. *Courtesy of the Kentucky Humanities Council.*

World War II

Clarke marker.
Courtesy of the author.

Trowbridge does not know if Clarke intended to make army history. But he said she did. So does a state historical society marker on the courthouse lawn in Lawrenceburg.

"While stationed at Douglas Air Field, Arizona, she led fight to desegregate base theater," the metal plaque says. "She was first black WAAC assigned to duty with an all-white company as platoon commander."

Haley S. Bowling also commemorates Clarke's life by portraying her in the Kentucky Humanities Council Chautauqua series, a program in which actors portray figures from Kentucky history. "I think there are people who are born with the drive and confidence to see things through," said Bowling, who lives in McKee. "But I can't believe how young she was and how dynamic she was when she accomplished all she did."

Clarke died of a ruptured appendix in 1944. She was twenty-four.

Clarke grew up in Jim Crow Kentucky when African Americans were kept separate and unequal from whites. The military was racially segregated, too.

"Ultimately, though, Clarke decided the army offered her a better life than the civilian world," Trowbridge said.

After graduating from Lawrenceburg's black high school in 1937, Clarke enrolled at Kentucky State. She earned a bachelor's degree in sociology and economics, Trowbridge said.

Bethune was a well-known educator and civil rights leader when she spoke at Kentucky State. "She was also considered the 'surrogate mother' of the black WAACs," said Trowbridge, who lives in Lawrenceburg.

Clarke completed basic training and officer training at Fort Des Moines, Iowa, and was commissioned a second lieutenant on February 16, 1943. She also got her photograph taken with a famous visitor.

"First Lady Eleanor Roosevelt," Bowling said. "She was also an inspiration to Anna Mac Clarke."

Though Fort Des Moines was far from the Jim Crow South, post facilities were segregated. "The officers' club was off limits to black officers," Trowbridge said. "So was the swimming pool, except for one hour on Friday evenings. Immediately after the blacks used the pool, the water underwent cleaning."

Also in February 1943, Clarke cracked the color bar and helped make WAAC history. "She became the first black WAAC to command an all-white platoon," Trowbridge said.

After serving elsewhere stateside, Clarke was back at Fort Des Moines in September 1943, when the Women's Auxiliary Army Corps became the Women's Army Corps. She was promoted to first lieutenant.

The Kentuckian successfully fought an army decision to create an all-African American WAC regiment. Trowbridge compared the plan to apartheid in white-ruled South Africa.

"Clarke and the other black officers felt a segregated regiment was counter to everything the United States was supposed to be fighting for in the war. The army rescinded the plan before it was implemented."

Clarke never married. But while stationed at Chico Army Air Field near Chico, California, a GI from back home came calling. "Chester Gill Jr., who was from Lawrenceburg, was stationed at the base," Trowbridge said. "He walked up to her, saluted and asked her if it was okay for enlisted men to date female officers. She said no. He saluted, did an about face and left her standing there."

Clarke continued to battle discrimination at Douglas Army Air Field, Arizona, near Tucson. Soon after she and other African American WACs arrived, black servicemen asked them to boycott the movie theater because it was segregated. "Clarke and other African American WACs did go to the theater but refused to sit in the black section," Trowbridge said.

World War II

Clarke also protested all the way up the chain of command. On February 21, 1944, Colonel Harvey E. Dyer, the base commander, issued an order declaring that "the colored officers are entitled to all the courtesies and privileges extended to white officers and the colored enlisted women are entitled to all of the courtesies and privileges extended to white enlisted men and women...Every consideration, respect, courtesy and toleration will be afforded every colored WAC. No discrimination will be condoned."

Dyer added,

> *"These colored WACs are citizens of the United States, imbued with a spirit of patriotism which prompted them to enlist in the Women's Army Corps as their contribution toward the war effort. They are comparatively well educated, of good moral character and possess high ideals. They are proud to serve their country, these great United States of America, in the capacity of women soldiers. They deserve our greatest respect."*

Clarke's stand made newspaper headlines nationwide. "It was another step on the road to ending segregation and discrimination in the military," Trowbridge said.

Clarke even was written up in the *Thorobred*, her college newspaper. "She had worked on the paper when she was at Kentucky State," Trowbridge said. "*The Thorobred* said she was 'really doing all right in the WAC. She moved up to 1st lieutenant fast and now we hear she's preparing for a captaincy.'"

The captaincy never came. One day, Clarke reported to the base hospital after suffering pain in her lower right abdomen. Doctors examined her; their diagnosis was grim. Her appendix had burst.

Surgeons removed her appendix, but gangrene had developed. "At first, they thought she might recover, but the gangrene was too severe," Trowbridge said.

Clark died on April 19, 1944, and her body was sent home by train. Clarke was buried in Woodlawn Hills Cemetery in the Stringtown community.

Trowbridge said:

> *Fifty years after her death, Anna Mac Clarke was remembered by friends, family and the Kentucky Historical Society when she was included in the "Praise the Lord and Pass the Ammunition: Kentuckians and World War II" exhibit and catalog which told Kentucky's World War II story...In 1995, Ms. Etta Withrow submitted her name and story to Washington, D.C., to be included in the "Women in Military Service for America Memorial Foundation, Inc."*

> *Anna Mac Clarke was a pioneer, part of a unique group of women who came together for one purpose—to help their country win a world war. She and her sister WAACs would also fight another war at home; that of racism, and they, as one unified force, began to break down the barriers of race and gender which would eventually lead to the civil rights movement of the late 1940s, up through the 1960s. Anna Mac would never know the full impact her efforts to right wrongs would have on things that we take for granted today, not only in the military, but in the civilian world as well.*

"I Don't Remember What the General Said—'Thanks,' I Guess"

When Charlie Oates started his Madisonville doughnut shop, he proudly put up a photo of his first "customer."

"He wasn't actually a customer," Oates hedged. "He was the first person I ever served a doughnut."

The photo was snapped in a London, England GI club, where an army major asked Corporal Charles K. Oates if he would hand a doughnut to a VIP. "They wanted some PR pictures," said Oates, who was an army air force clerk, not a pastry chef. "But he was a major, and I was a corporal. So I said, 'Sure, I'll do it.'"

The VIP happened to be General Dwight D. Eisenhower. A photo of Oates offering Ike a doughnut was splashed on the front page of the GI paper, *Stars and Stripes*.

"When the photo also ran in a London newspaper, the Associated Press picked it up," Oates said. "It ran in papers all over the United States, too."

The story didn't end there. After Oates was discharged in 1945, he returned home determined to go into the doughnut business.

Oates wrote the Downyflake Doughnut Company about starting a local franchise. "A representative of the company came to town," Oates said. "While he was giving me the company line, he pulled a photograph out of his case and said the company was using it for publicity."

It was Oates offering Ike a bite. "I asked the guy, 'Do you recognize the corporal in the picture?' He looked at the photo, then at me and did a double-take." When the ex-corporal started Oates Grill and Doughnut Shop in 1946, he and Ike went up over the counter.

Oates met the general in the Washington Club, a London hotel the Red Cross turned into a hangout for Americans in Britain. It was the Fourth of July 1942.

Oates and a buddy were in town on a three-day pass. Word spread that Eisenhower was dropping by the club.

"They wanted us to go to the ballroom to greet him," Oates said. No sooner had he walked in than a major handed him a stick of three doughnuts and told him to offer Eisenhower one. "I don't remember what the general said—'thanks,' I guess. But he took a bite for the *Stars and Stripes* photographer and another one for a London newspaper photographer."

Oates said he never again crossed paths with Eisenhower, who went on to become supreme Allied commander in Europe and president in 1953.

But the corporal and the doughnut-munching brass hat made headlines again. Oates, the photo and the story behind it were featured in *American Heritage* magazine.

Despite his famous first "customer," Oates was in the doughnut business only briefly. "I sold the grill after two years," he said with a chuckle. "It was too much work. So I started selling real estate."

"Cool Determination and Seemingly Utter Disregard for His Own Life"

The navy named a destroyer escort for a Paducah hero who gave his life defending the USS *San Francisco* against an attacking Japanese torpedo bomber in the 1942 Battle of Guadalcanal.

Gunner's Mate Harry James Loe Jr. was posthumously awarded the Navy Cross for valor. The USS *Lowe*, commissioned in 1943, bore his name, which the navy spelled "Lowe."

The 9,950-ton *San Francisco*, a heavy cruiser, was part of a force of American warships that bombarded Japanese shore batteries on strategic Guadalcanal the day Lowe died. It was November 12.

Lowe's battle station was a 20 mm rapid-firing antiaircraft gun. He kept shooting even as an attacking Japanese torpedo bomber flew straight toward him, preparing to launch its deadly steel fish.

"The plane kept coming in, directly in line with Lowe's fire but the Paducahan stood his ground," the *Paducah Sun-Democrat* reported. "He refused to run away from his station after it was inevitable that the torpedo would hit the ship" if the enemy's aim was straight.

The sailor's hometown paper added, "Lowe, with cool determination and seemingly utter disregard for his own life, sent a well placed hunk of steel from his hot gun into the diving plane. It shuddered, then crashed with a burst of fire into the battle station."

Besides Lowe, whom the *Sun-Democrat* described as "a blonde slender kid who was always laughing," the crash killed twenty-nine other sailors, according to navy reports.

Lowe also received a posthumous Purple Heart. The navy sent both medals to Lowe's mother and father, Celia and Harry James Loe Sr.

The USS *Lowe*—officially DE (for Destroyer Escort) 325—was launched at a shipyard in Orange, Texas, on July 28, 1943. Celia Loe broke the traditional champagne bottle over the ship's bow in christening ceremonies.

The *Lowe* did not battle the Japanese. The sleek, fast 306-foot-long warship saw duty in the Atlantic Ocean. The *Lowe* helped escort convoys to North Africa in 1944, and in March 1945, it was credited with sinking a German submarine near Halifax, Nova Scotia.

In 1962, the ship was on call to rescue astronaut John Glenn, the first American to orbit the earth, in case his space capsule crashed into the sea. After service in the Vietnam conflict, the *Lowe* was decommissioned in 1968 and scrapped.

"They Fought for Their Lives Against Sharklike Fighter Planes"

Daniel "Snooty" Johnson remembers the German fighter plane that didn't get away.

"The pilot did; he bailed out," Johnson said. "He'd just finished his firing pass and was peeling off when I got him. There wasn't any smoke or fire. The plane just went into a spin. It was my fifth mission—January 11, 1944."

Staff Sergeant Johnson's sharp shooting from the ball turret of a B-17 bomber earned him a second Air Medal. The duel was high above Oschersleben, Germany. The bombers' target was enemy aircraft factories.

Johnson came home from World War II and worked as a construction pipefitter for brother Clifton "Pip" Johnson's construction company in Symsonia, in Graves County. Snooty belonged to Plumbers and Steamfitters Local 184 in Paducah.

In 1943–1944, he flew thirty-five combat missions against targets in Nazi-ruled Europe. The Graves Countian also won a Distinguished Flying Cross, a Presidential Unit Citation and four Air Medals.

"In few instances in the varied, far-flung combat of World War II were heroism and tragedy more concentrated and starkly interwoven than in the flights of the big bombers," wrote historian Charles B. MacDonald in his

World War II

Johnson, third from left, and crew. *Courtesy of Daniel Johnson.*

book, *The Mighty Endeavor: American Armed Forces in the European Theater in World War II*. "Engaged on missions of death, they fought for their lives against sharklike fighter planes hungry for the kill."

Johnson had probably the toughest and most perilous job on a U.S. heavy bomber. "A ball turret wasn't built for comfort," said Johnson, grinning. "I was rolled up pretty good."

It was no joke. In flight, he spent many hours wedged inside the tiny plexiglass globe on the belly of the B-17. "I'd get in about halfway across the English Channel. I didn't get out until we were in about the same place going home."

Johnson was a skinny, five-foot, eight-inch-tall man. He weighed just 130 pounds. Even so, it was such a tight fit in the turret that he couldn't wear a lifesaving parachute. "I did have a harness over my flight suit, but had to leave the 'chute up in the plane."

The ball turret was also jammed with twin .50-caliber machine guns and belts of ammunition. "The only way out was through the plane," Johnson said. "But if the plane got hit and we went into a spin, you'd be pinned inside the turret and more than likely never get out."

Snooty Johnson—nobody calls him Daniel—joined the 351st Bomb Group, part of the 8th Air Force, in Polebrook, England, in November 1943. He was twenty years old.

Johnson and nine other fliers, all rookies, were assigned to a bomber their pilot, First Lieutenant Sterling L. McCluskey, christened April Girl II for another B-17 the Germans had shot down. "His wife was expecting a baby girl in April," Johnson said with a chuckle. "When she had a boy, the rest of us said he should have named the plane 'April Fool.'"

April Girl II got its baptism of fire on November 26, 1943, when the 351st struck Bremen, Germany. Antiaircraft gunners greeted the Americans with a wall of flak. "None of us had ever seen flak before," Johnson said. "But there it was—this flash, then a puff of black smoke. None of us got hurt that time, but there were plenty of holes in the plane."

Johnson said he soon learned that when antiaircraft fire slackened around a target, it didn't mean the bombers were safe. "When they let up, you could bet the German fighters weren't far behind."

As many as 150 Nazi fighters swarmed on the 351st over Oschersleben. "They really threw everything at us. We fired every round of .50-caliber ammunition we had in the plane and me and the tail gunner shot the rifling out of our machine gun barrels—burned 'em plum up."

In the melee, Johnson drew a quick bead on a twin-engine Messerschmitt 110. The pilot darted at April Girl II, fired his 20 and 30 mm cannons, missed and tried to turn away. But a well-aimed burst from Johnson's machine guns dispatched the enemy.

He saw the pilot jump free, but not the rear gunner. "I got that one!" Johnson yelled on the interphone as the plane spiraled downward. "Good, get the rest of 'em," McCluskey replied.

"That was the only plane I got credit for shooting down in the war, but I didn't watch it fall far," Johnson said. "There were too many other targets."

April Girl II made it back to Polebrook. But enemy fighters destroyed six other B-17s in the twenty-two-bomber Oschersleben raid.

Before his combat tour ended in 1944, Johnson flew on even larger raids against Hamburg, Frankfurt and other cities, including Berlin, the Nazi capital. "We hit a long string of oil storage tanks in Hamburg [on April 8, 1944]. It seemed like the flames rose up so high they almost touched our plane."

The next day, the 351st pounded Rahmal, Germany, and flew near Hamburg. "You could see big thick clouds of smoke over those oil tanks that were still burning," Johnson said.

He and the rest of April Girl II's crew earned a special commendation for the Rahmal raid. Brigadier General Robert B. Williams cited the airmen "for the outstanding teamwork which they displayed in assuring the success of this attack."

All told, the 351st Bomb Group flew 311 combat missions in World War II and dropped 20,778 tons of bombs on enemy targets. The group's air gunners were credited with shooting down 303 enemy fighters, according to the 351st Bomb Group's website.

Even so, German fighters and antiaircraft guns took a heavy toll in 351st men and machines. The group lost 124 B-17s in combat, the website says. Many fliers were killed, wounded or captured.

Johnson's whole crew made it through the war, even though flak wounded April Girl II's co-pilot twice. "Once in the left leg and once in the head," he said.

April Girl II was a survivor as well, returning stateside in 1945. "I don't know if they scrapped her or what happened to her," Johnson said. "But she flew a total of 113 missions. That must have been a record in our group, or close to it."

Snooty Johnson came home to Symsonia in 1945. He married his sweetheart, Freda Clapp.

Johnson was one of six sons of Frank and Ida Johnson who fought in World War II. Glenn, Ulus, Clifton and Ira also survived. Carl Johnson, a marine private, was killed on Iwo Jima in 1945. He was nineteen.

"When I Smelled My Hair Burning, It Gave Me the Strength to Live"

Chester W. "Bill" Hack of Paducah had survived bloody air combat and the fiery crash of a B-17 bomber into the English Channel.

He was back stateside teaching aerial gunnery in sunny Florida, where he said he lost his mind. "I volunteered to go back and fly combat missions again."

Nazi fighters and antiaircraft fire blasted Hack's bomber from the sky on May 29, 1943. "When we ditched in the channel, I was dazed," Hack said. "But when I smelled my hair burning, it gave me the strength to live."

Hack was twenty-two the day he nearly died. It was his third mission against the Germans in a B-17. The plane Hack was aboard was nicknamed Barrel House Bessie by its crew.

"I think there was a song about Barrel House Bessie from Basin Street in New Orleans," said Hack, who after the war worked for fifty-three years out of Paducah Ironworkers Local 782, retiring as business agent.

Bill Hack. *Photo by the author.*

Hack's plane took off with the Chelveston, England–based 305th "Can Do" Bomb Group. The bombers' destination was the German submarine base at St. Nazaire, France, on the Atlantic Ocean. There were so many antiaircraft guns around St. Nazaire that the American fliers dubbed the seaport Flak City.

World War II

Bill Hack in uniform. *Courtesy of Bill Hack.*

Few targets were tougher than the U-boat pens. Each was roofed with tons of steel-reinforced concrete. The Germans boasted the pens were impregnable.

When Hack reported to the 305th group, American heavy bomber crews had to complete twenty-five missions before they could go home. A flier's chance of reaching the magic number was one in three, according to Hack. "Most of us just resigned ourselves to knowing we were going to get shot down," he said. "The only question was would you be killed, or would you be able to bail out, then be captured or rescued."

On the St. Nazaire raid, Hack was Bessie's right-waist gunner, manning a .50-caliber machine gun about halfway along the B-17's pudgy, round fuselage. The western Kentuckian arrived from England as part of a crew he trained with stateside.

"A B-17 had ten men," Hack said. "The crew included the pilot, co-pilot, navigator and bombardier, radio operator, flight engineer-top turret gunner, two waist gunners, a ball turret gunner and a tail gunner."

Hack usually flew in another B-17 with "Me and My Gal" painted on its nose. "Our radioman named the plane for a song Judy Garland sang that went, 'The Bells Are Ringing for Me and My Gal,'" Hack said, grinning. "He was kind of stuck on Judy Garland."

Hack was on loan to Barrel House Bessie for the St. Nazaire raid. He was filling in for a gunner killed in action a few days before.

Hack and Bessie's other gunners had plenty to shoot at en route to St. Nazaire. Speedy cannon and machine-gun firing Messerschmitt 109 and Focke Wulf 190 fighters bushwhacked the lumbering bomb-laden warplanes dubbed Flying Fortresses. "We were under attack all the way from the English Channel into St. Nazaire," he said.

Bessie took a beating but kept flying. "The plane was shot up pretty badly before we even got to the target," Hack said.

A 20 mm cannon shell from a Focke Wulf tore through the fuselage, missing Hack's head by inches and slicing his life-sustaining oxygen line in two.

Hack reached down for his metal emergency bottle, which held a thirty-minute supply of oxygen. "As I worked to plug my oxygen mask into it, a shell hit the bottle, and it blew up in my hands. By this time, I was so weak from lack of oxygen that I was down on my knees.

"I crawled to the left waist gunner, got him by the leg and pointed to my mask. He immediately grabbed his emergency bottle and plugged me into it. I got to feeling better."

Hack's comfort was fleeting. "Flak was real heavy over St. Nazaire. The sky looked like a big black cloud from all that flak. I got wounded in the shoulder. Everybody on the plane was hit."

Bessie was hit hardest shortly after it dropped its bombs. A big flak barrage crippled Hack's plane and destroyed two B-17s flying with it. "We were in

World War II

three-plane formations," Hack said. "We were stacked three here, three there. The two with us blew up.

"Each one of them had some good friends of mine in it. I learned later that four of them bailed out, but two of them died that night in a German hospital. We lost a total of thirteen planes on the raid."

Flak riddled Bessie's number two engine, setting it ablaze. The B-17 nosed into what seemed to be a death dive.

"'This is it' crossed my mind," he said. "But I'd been feeling like 'this is it' for quite a while. We were in a very steep dive—from twenty-eight thousand feet to about five hundred feet—before the pilot and co-pilot were able to pull us out."

Hack said they were lucky the flak found Bessie after its bombs were away. "If that bomb load had gone off, we would have been vaporized. I have seen that happen, too, with other aircraft."

Once the pilots righted the wounded bomber, everything that could be spared was tossed overboard to lighten Bessie and keep it flying. Meanwhile, Hack checked on Sergeant Ralph Erwin, the tail gunner. "There were big holes all over the tail section. One was two feet in diameter. Ralph was hurt pretty bad. It looked like he was in shock."

Hack dragged Erwin to the radio room and then took over the twin .50-caliber machine guns, the stinger in Bessie's tail. Limping on three engines, the Fortress was not out of harm's way.

"When a plane is knocked out of formation like we were, the German fighters would gang on it like a pack of wolves. We had made it back to the French coast on the channel, about one hundred miles from England, when two Messerschmitts jumped us."

Hack squeezed off several bursts of rapid fire at the attackers. "I guess they thought they had a sitting duck," he said.

Suddenly, the Nazi planes turned tail and veered off toward France. Hack could hardly believe he had chased them away.

"I didn't," he said. "I looked up and saw a flight of British Spitfires. Those Spitfires were the most beautiful airplanes I ever saw. I felt like cheering."

Bessie still wasn't home free. "Our pilot, Lieutenant James Stevenson, had thought he could get us back to England, but 'Barrel House Bessie' had given us all she had."

Bessie was bound for a watery grave. "We were within fifty miles of the coast of England when we ditched," Hack said.

"The pilot told us to take what we called 'ditch positions.' We knew it was going to be rough. You could see whitecaps. We all got in the radio room and braced ourselves against the bulkhead walls."

Bessie slammed into the choppy sea. The impact hurled Hack and another crewman from the radio compartment through an aluminum door into the empty bomb bay.

"It knocked the door completely off its hinges," Hack said. "I thought my back was broken. The bomb bay was filling up with water and there was burning gas from the engines on top of it. The entire bomb bay was engulfed in flames."

Hack splashed sea water on his burning face and hair. Dazed, bruised and bleeding, he managed to flee the bomber before it sank. "By the time I got back into the radio room, the rest of the crew had gotten out," he said. Hack escaped by wiggling through a window in the top of the plane above the radio operator's seat.

He slid down the fuselage onto the right wing. "Fire had completely encircled the plane and the gasoline was spreading all over the water," Hack said.

Bessie carried a pair of inflatable rubber dinghies. One was banged up, the other burned up.

Hack plunged into the frigid salt water and swam through the blazing gasoline to reach the damaged dinghy. "It had been shot full of holes and couldn't be fully inflated," he said.

Everybody but Ralph Erwin got out of Barrel House Bessie, which soon slipped beneath the sea. "We couldn't get into the raft—we inflated it to a cigar shape—but nine of us held on to it for an hour and a half," Hack said.

As the Spitfires circled overhead protecting their American allies from more German fighters, a British seaplane arrived to rescue the downed fliers. But the channel was too rough for a landing, and the flying boat turned back to England. "That was really hard to take to see him disappearing," Hack said.

Meanwhile, he and the other fliers watched helplessly as Erwin's lifeless body floated farther away. "Ralph was thirty-one, from Dallas, Oregon. He was a quiet guy who didn't much mix with the rest of us, but we all liked him."

Having survived enemy fighters, flak, a near-death dive and a crash landing in the wave-tossed sea, Bessie's crew faced yet another peril. "Hypothermia," Hack said. "They told me that even in the month of May, the English Channel is usually around forty-eight degrees.

"We had just about succumbed when a British navy torpedo boat finally got to us." The nine Americans were hauled safely aboard the little boat, which bobbed like a cork in the heavy sea.

The fliers asked the British captain to retrieve Erwin's body. "But he said we had to leave him because of the danger of enemy air attacks," Hack said. "So we left Ralph, and he floated away into oblivion."

World War II

Hack said he was so numb from the cold sea "that they had to tie a rope around me and pull me up on the deck. I couldn't climb that rope ladder on the boat.

"I was sprawled out on the deck and a British sailor—I never will forget him, God bless him—stuck this bottle of rum in my mouth. It was either drink or drown. I didn't have the strength to push it away.

"He just kept pouring that rum in me. I don't know if it was from shock, hypothermia or that rum, but I passed out, and when I came to I was in an ambulance on the way to a British naval hospital."

After two weeks in British and U.S. military hospitals, Hack was back with his bomber group. He rejoined his old crew, what was left of them. "Four of the ten had been killed," Hack said. Still, he was glad to be reunited with his buddies and Me and My Gal.

Hack logged twenty-two more missions, including the Eighth Air Force's famous first raid on heavily defended Schweinfurt and Regensburg, Germany, one of the bloodiest air battles of the war. It was August 17, 1943.

Schweinfurt was home to ball bearing factories. The enemy built Messerschmitt fighters at Regensburg. The 305th's target was Schweinfurt.

"The Regensburg-Schweinfurt mission was historic, too, because it marked the deepest [Eighth Air Force] penetration into Germany to that time," wrote Edward M. Jablonski in *Flying Fortress: The Illustrated Biography of the B-17s and the Men Who Flew Them.* The raid "employed the largest force dispatched—376 Flying Fortresses," he added.

"They told us before we left that not many of us would be coming back from this one," Hack said. "But they said if we destroyed those ball bearing plants, it would really hurt the Germans and save untold lives of our soldiers on the ground."

Hack said Nazi fighters and flak made the blue sky "look like a junkyard—a plane's wing blown off over here, an engine over there, a tail section someplace else and six guys going past with their parachutes on fire. It was horrible."

Miraculously, his plane was only slightly damaged. Many more crews were not so fortunate. According to army air force records, sixty bombers were shot down.

After mission twenty-five, Hack was shipped stateside. He returned to air combat in early 1945 and flew against the Nazis four more times before the war in Europe ended in May 1945. He said his happiest mission of the war was over Holland that spring. He was in a group of B-17s that flew low and dropped food to starving Dutch civilians.

Staff Sergeant Hack, who had lived with his family in Detroit before the war, moved back to Paducah after he was discharged. His service to his country earned him a Distinguished Flying Cross, a Purple Heart, four Air Medals and two Presidential Unit Citations.

"To the Gates of Hell"

An old torpedo mounted on a concrete pedestal in downtown Owensboro memorializes "the most well-known submarine commanding officer of the war" and the crew of "the most famous U.S. submarine of World War II."

The steel fish is harmless, unlike the USS *Wahoo*'s TNT-packed torpedoes. While Owensboro native "Mush" Morton was its skipper for most of 1943, the long-range fleet sub sank at least nineteen Japanese ships before the enemy got even.

The monument was erected in 1994, almost fifty-one years after the *Wahoo* and its crew were lost in action to a Japanese warplane. The memorial is on the lawn of the local American Legion post.

"The USS *Wahoo* is, according to most informed sources, the most famous U.S. submarine of World War II, and 'Mush' Morton is the most well-known

Morton monument. *Courtesy of the author.*

submarine commander of the war," a 2006 *Owensboro Messenger-Inquirer* story quoted Charles R. Hinman, director of education and outreach for both the USS *Bowfin* Submarine Museum & Park in Hawaii and the *Wahoo* Project Group.

Hinman added, "In the final totals, the boat and her skipper did not have the greatest record in terms of ships and tonnage sunk, but the influence of the aggressive Commander Morton on the U.S. Submarine Force is unquestionably of the highest order." By the war's end, according to Hinman, U.S. subs "had accounted for approximately 55 percent of the enemy vessels sunk in the Pacific, more than all other forces combined."

"Morton," the *Messenger-Inquirer* story by Keith Lawrence explained, "is credited with being the first U.S. submariner to penetrate an enemy harbor and sink an enemy ship within it, the first to challenge a ship head-on in a 'down-the-throat' maneuver and the first to single-handedly wipe out an entire convoy."

His bravery did not go unrewarded. The Kentuckian earned four Navy Crosses and an army Distinguished Service Cross.

The son of a coal miner, Morton was born in Owensboro, the Daviess County seat, in 1907. When he was about ten years old, the family moved to nearby Nortonville, then to Miami where the future sub skipper went to high school, Lawrence wrote.

Morton enrolled in the U.S. Naval Academy at Annapolis in 1926. According to navy legend, he picked up the nickname "Mushmouth," later shortened to "Mush," because of his Kentucky accent, Lawrence added.

"They called me Mushmouth when I was a plebe at the Academy and the name Mush has stuck with me since," wrote Associated Press war correspondent Walter Clausen in a 1943 dispatch published in the *Owensboro Messenger*. "And my real action started off Musha Island, New Guinea, so we called it Mush Harbor."

Promoted to commander on October 15, 1942, Morton took over the *Wahoo* on December 31. "Between Jan. 26 and Oct. 11, 1943, the *Wahoo* is credited with sinking 19 cargo and transport ships for a combined total of 55,000 tons," Lawrence wrote.

Clausen filed his story from "a Pacific Base" where the *Wahoo* returned after sinking eight Japanese vessels. "This fleet submarine has…a broom attached to its periscope to indicate a clean sweep and flies a pennant with eight Japanese flags fluttering beneath to denote a bag of two combat ships and six auxiliaries," he wrote.

Clausen added:

> *The broom was in token of the complete wiping out of a Japanese convoy north of Central New Guinea. One of these torpedoed ships was fully loaded with an estimated 1,500 to 6,000…troops bound for Wewak, some 300 miles northwest of Salamaua, to establish a new platform against the advances of General* [Douglas] *MacArthur's forces in New Guinea.*

The *Wahoo* sank one of the enemy ships in Musha Harbor. "A few weeks after leaving our base we were looking for Wewak harbor and couldn't find it on our charts, but one of the crew dug up a 25-cent atlas which had it and we made a chart from it," Clausen quoted Morton. "We thought it was Wewak harbor, but it proved to be Finger Bay, Musha Island. We discovered a ship deep in the narrow harbor and found it to be a destroyer, apparently taking on water and anchored."

As the unseen *Wahoo* closed on the target, the destroyer weighed anchor and began steaming out of the harbor. "But instead of turning our way it turned south," Morton told Clausen. "We sent four torpedoes after it. They missed. It was the first evidence that the destroyer knew we were there when it saw the torpedoes coming, and the destroyer came charging after us at 20 knots."

Morton said the aroused enemy was only eight hundred yards away when he fired his last torpedo. "We were headed for each other," he added.

There was a collision, but it was between the *Wahoo*'s torpedo and the Japanese warship, which had veered away at the last minute. "At 500 yards it smacked amidships and the explosion was so terrific we did not know but what we had been hit," Morton recalled.

Even so, there was fight left in the victim of Morton's famous "down the throat" shot. "Although disabled and cut in two, with the bow sinking, it fired on us and we hightailed it out. That was January 24."

Two days later, the *Wahoo* encountered a convoy of four Japanese vessels. "These were headed, we believe, for Wewak," he told Clausen. "We found them about 240 miles north of Wewak. Early in the morning we contacted them and chased them until noon."

The *Wahoo* torpedoed and sank the lead ship, a freighter and the one behind it, a transport. Each was about seven thousand tons, according to Morton, who said his sub damaged a third ship that tried to escape.

"The transport was fully loaded with troops," the sub skipper said.

World War II

> *We figured there were at least 1,500 aboard but later were led to believe there must have been 6,000...After the torpedoing the ships engaged in battle with us but we destroyed them.*
>
> *In fact, it was a fourteen hour battle that day before we finished the convoy. After finishing the first two we chased the third and about sunset caught it and destroyed it. At 9 o'clock that night we caught the fourth ship, a tanker, and sent it to the bottom.*

On January 27, the *Wahoo* crossed paths with a six-ship Japanese convoy that Morton figured was bound for Rabaul, New Britain. "We had no torpedoes left but went after them with a surface gun attack," Morton said. "It was 10 o'clock in the morning. The ships opened fire on us with everything they had."

A destroyer joined the fray, training its guns on the *Wahoo*. The Americans "were running" and the Japanese were "gunning," Morton said. "It is a sort of helpless feeling when you have no torpedoes. The destroyers look small when you are attacking them, but plenty big when they come after you. It charged in at thirty knots and we went below. We were not harmed."

Morton and the *Wahoo* stayed unharmed on three war patrols until the captain and his crew were given their toughest assignment: hunting enemy ships in the Sea of Japan. "When he didn't return, the *Wahoo* was reported missing that December," Lawrence wrote.

The hometown *Messenger* relayed the sad news to its readers with a page-one AP dispatch from Washington headlined "Dudley Walker Morton Missing with Heroic Submarine *Wahoo*." The story said, "The heroic submarine... which even the Axis admits was daring enough to sink Japanese ships at the rate of one a month," has fired its last shots.

Lawrence wrote that after the war, the navy determined from Japanese records that on October 11, 1943—the day the *Wahoo* was to exit the Sea of Japan—"an antisubmarine aircraft discovered it on the surface and attacked, dropping three depth charges." The submarine sank in the La Perouse Strait.

The navy waited until January 7, 1946, to declare Morton and the *Wahoo*'s crew dead officially, according to Lawrence.

"Technically, there were no survivors, although retired navy chief yeoman Forest J. Sterling certainly considers himself one," Stewart Jennison wrote in the *Messenger-Inquirer*. Sterling, of Gulfport, Mississippi, had expected to be aboard the sub on its last patrol "but received an offer to return to the United States before the *Wahoo* began its...fateful mission."

The old sailor was an honored guest for the dedication of the monument, which overlooks the Ohio River. Sterling told about watching the submarine leave on its final patrol in *Wake of the Wahoo*, his memoirs, which were published in 1960.

The book includes a foreword written by Vice Admiral Charles A. Lockwood Jr., commander of U.S. submarines in the Pacific during World War II. "When a natural leader and born daredevil such as Mush Morton is given command of a submarine, the result can only be a fighting ship of the highest order, with officers and men who would follow their skipper to the Gates of Hell…And they did," he wrote.

Mayfield Sailor Is Memorialized at Normandy Cemetery

Shadrach Boaz of Mayfield went down with his landing craft off Omaha Beach on D-Day.

"His body was never found," said Sam Boaz of Paducah, the ensign's brother. Shadrach Boaz died at age twenty-three.

Normandy Cemetery. *Courtesy of the author.*

World War II

Boaz memorial stone.
Courtesy of the author.

Ensign Boaz was not forgotten by his family or by his country. A stout block of white marble honors the sailor on the Boaz plot at Highland Park Cemetery in Mayfield.

The western Kentuckian is also remembered in the Garden of the Missing, part of the Normandy American Cemetery and Memorial near Colleville-sur-Mer. The hallowed ground carpeted with neatly mowed Kentucky bluegrass overlooks "Bloody Omaha" and the English Channel.

The names of Boaz and 1,556 other U.S. soldiers, sailors and airmen are chiseled on the gray stone Wall of the Missing. Another 9,387 military dead from D-Day and other World War II battles are buried beneath white marble Latin Crosses and Stars of David in the cemetery, where the opening scene of the popular movie *Saving Private Ryan* was filmed.

Time and tides have washed away the blood of 2,200 Americans who were killed or wounded at Omaha Beach, a four-mile stretch of Normandy sand and sea-smoothed pebbles. Heavily defended Omaha was the deadliest of the five Allied invasion beaches on D-Day, June 6, 1944.

Below the cliff-top cemetery, the U.S. First Infantry Division—the storied "Big Red One"—stormed ashore against the Germans. Part of the Twenty-ninth Infantry Division and Army Rangers battled the enemy on the western end of Omaha Beach. "My brother was on an LCT, a Landing Craft Tank," said Boaz, an attorney.

Shadrach Boaz was a veteran of U.S. landings in North Africa and Italy. "Then he was sent to England for D-Day," Sam Boaz said.

LCTs were crewed by two officers and fourteen to fifteen sailors for the Normandy invasion, the largest amphibious attack in history. Each sturdy steel boat—32 feet wide and 119 feet long—could carry four to eight tanks or self-propelled guns and beach them via a bow ramp.

On D-Day, Boaz was assistant officer in charge of LCT 197, part of Flotilla 18. The boat was to land self-propelled guns and gunners of the Fifty-eighth Armored Field Artillery in support of the Twenty-ninth Infantry, according to a July 10, 1944 navy report describing the loss of LCT 197.

Boaz's craft tried to land at 10:00 a.m. "but was prevented from doing so by underwater obstacles and heavy fire," explained the report, written by Lieutenant Commander A. Hays, Flotilla 18 commander. LCT 197 struck a mine, which exploded.

"Terrific concussions were felt aboard, and the seams of the craft were split open," Hays added. "The after section began to fill with water and the craft listed badly to port."

The blast knocked out two of LCT 197's three diesel engines. The landing craft limped toward a repair tug as the crew manned hand pumps to keep the boat afloat. Sailors on the tug tried to save LCT 197 with their larger pumps. "After ninety minutes of pumping, the repair tug was ordered to another area," the report says.

Undaunted, LCT 197's skipper, Ensign W. Whitney, tried to reach the beach three more times, but to no avail. "All attempts to secure aid were futile," the report said.

Whitney was determined at least to save the soldiers and their much-needed firepower. He turned the LCT seaward to transfer its cargo to a larger Landing Ship Tank, an LST in navy lingo. The soldiers got off, the report said, but without their big guns, each of which was mounted on a tank chassis.

Finally, at 8:35 p.m., LCT 197's lone working engine sputtered to a stop.

"The afterdeck on the port side was inundated," the report stated. Twenty minutes later, "the ship was abandoned with its complete load aboard. The craft turned over to port almost immediately and sank slowly, approximately

World War II

four miles off Omaha Beach. One officer remains unaccounted for; all other personnel survived."

The missing officer was Ensign Shadrach Whitis Boaz, serial number 0-226983, United States Naval Reserve.

"Small-Town, Country Boy" Wondered If His First Dogfight Might Be His Last

Colonel Herschel H. "Herky" Green of Mayfield shot down a half-dozen enemy airplanes on just one mission in World War II.

He was piloting a borrowed plane and did not know he had more ammunition. Otherwise, he might have notched a higher tally. Even so, Green's flying feat has few parallels in the history of air combat. It is even chiseled in stone.

Green monument.
Courtesy of the author.

"On 30 January 1944 Colonel Green Shot Down 6 Aircraft in One Day," says the hero's shiny black granite monument on the Graves County courthouse lawn in Mayfield, his hometown. Green died in California in 2006 at age eighty-six.

The Kentucky native shot down eighteen Axis aircraft in 1943–1944. He was one of the few army air force pilots who were aces in two different fighters, the P-47 Thunderbolt and the P-51 Mustang.

Green, who also flew a P-40 Warhawk, won promotions and a chest full of decorations. He earned the Distinguished Service Cross, the Silver Star, two Distinguished Flying Crosses, twenty-six Air Medals, a Purple Heart, the Joint Services Commendation Medal and the French Croix de Guerre with Palm.

Green ended up commanding his outfit, the 317th Fighter Squadron of the 325th Fighter Group, dubbed the Checkertails because of bright yellow and black checkerboards painted on their planes' tails. He was the top U.S. ace in the Mediterranean Theater, when he was promoted to 15th Army Air Force headquarters in 1944 and had to stop flying.

Green made colonel before he left the air force in 1964. Afterward, he worked for Hughes Aircraft in California for eighteen years.

Green's monument is a local landmark. In 1992, former mayor John Boyd led a fund drive to get it built in honor of Green, who played trumpet in the band at Mayfield High School, where he graduated in 1937 at age seventeen.

Green went to Vanderbilt University in Nashville but left school for the army air force. The Graves Countian earned silver pilot's wings and gold second lieutenant's bars before he went overseas.

The famous air ace was all but forgotten in Mayfield, according to Boyd, a World War II army air force veteran and ex–prisoner of war. "Here we had this hero who shot down eighteen aircraft and got every medal you could think of except the Congressional Medal of Honor," Boyd said. "But a lot of people in Mayfield didn't even know who he was."

After the monument came state recognition for Green. In 2001, he was inducted into the Kentucky Aviation Hall of Fame in Lexington.

Green mostly flew from air bases in North Africa and Italy. He logged one hundred combat missions, none more fateful than the one on January 30, 1944.

Green's P-47 fighter was grounded for repairs. So he flew another P-47 in an attack on German airfields around Villaorba and Udine, Italy.

Green spotted four lumbering Junkers 52 triple-engine transports lined up, apparently for landing. Green got behind the trailing German plane and

World War II

shot it down. "I switched to the next plane, got off a quick burst setting it afire, and then switched to another, followed by a fourth, all with the same fatal results," he wrote in his illustrated autobiography, *Herky! The Memoirs of a Checkertail Ace*.

Seeking other targets, Green pounced on an Italian Macchi 202 fighter and destroyed it. (Italy, which had sided with Germany, pulled out of the war in 1943. While some Italians joined the Allies, others kept fighting in support of the Germans.)

Green's last kill was a German Dornier-217 twin-engine bomber. He set it on fire and watched it crash.

As he blasted the Nazi warplane, Green spied tracer rounds streaking from his eight wing-mounted, .50-caliber machine guns, a sign he was running out of ammunition. So he returned to his base.

Green thought he had four hundred rounds of ammo for each gun. He really had twice that amount.

The P-47 could haul 800 rounds per gun, Green explained. "Most of us, however, carried only 400 rounds…because we felt the weight reduction significantly improved aircraft performance," he wrote.

As a warning to pilots, 317th Squadron armorers would slip five tracer rounds onto the four-hundred-round ammunition belt when there were fifty shots left, Green said. Unknown to Green, the pilot whose plane he used flew with eight hundred rounds per gun.

The other pilot's armorer would snap two 400-round belts together, Green explained. "This meant that five tracers were fired just before the end of the first 400 rounds, as well as the second 400 rounds."

Had Green realized he had the extra firepower, he might have downed even more enemy aircraft on what was still his most productive mission.

Green wrote that he was thinking about Mayfield in his first dogfight, May 19, 1943. It looked like his last air combat.

Before he downed one enemy Messerschmitt 109, Green shook off two more but went into a spin in his bullet-riddled P-40 and almost crashed. Green nursed the crippled plane back to his base, where the fighter was junked.

"I knew that death was sitting in the cockpit with me," Green wrote. "There was no time for my life to pass before my eyes, but I did have time to wonder how in the world a small-town, country boy like me had gotten himself into such a mess."

Hidden History of Kentucky Soldiers

"It Felt Like a Hundred Hornets Were Stinging My Neck and Shoulder"

Staff Sergeant Bob Suitts flew thirty missions against German targets in World War II.

Suitts, who lives in Wingo, missed the 461st Bomb Group's raid on the Nazi tank works at Linz, Austria, on July 25, 1944. A serious flak wound grounded him and probably saved his life. But that is getting ahead of the story.

A Galesburg, Illinois native, Suitts was a nose turret gunner on big, four-engine B-24 Liberator bombers with nicknames like Spirit of '76 and Tail Dragon.

For the Linz attack, Sergeant Herbert Ellis of Brookline, Massachusetts, took Suitts's place behind the twin .50-caliber machine guns that bristled from Tail Dragon's stubby nose.

High over the Austrian city near where Adolf Hitler was born, a German Messerschmitt 262 jet fighter fired a rocket into Tail Dragon's right wing. The explosion flipped the olive-drab bomber and its ten-man crew upside down.

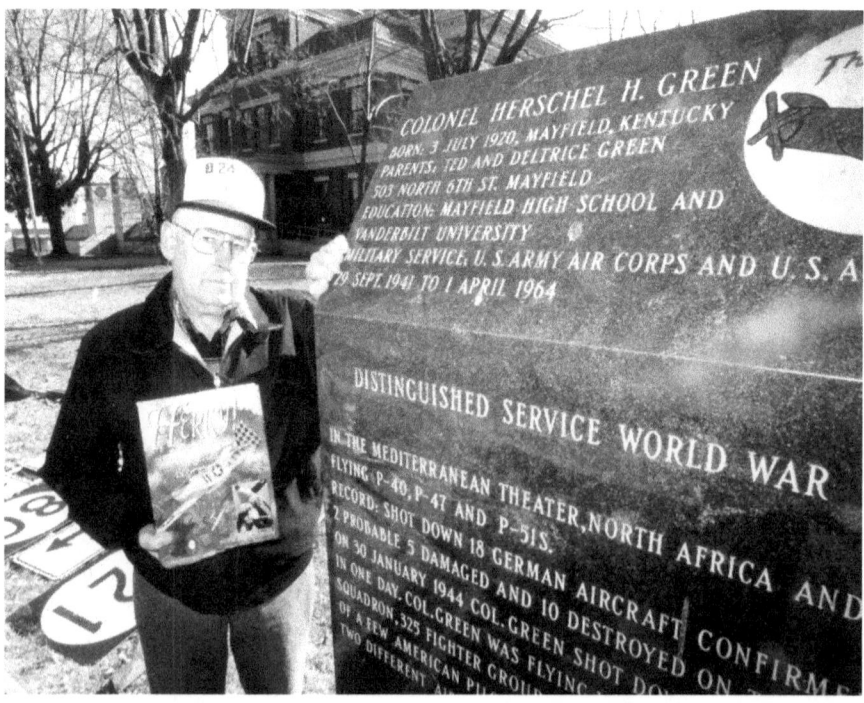

Bob Suitts. *Courtesy of the author.*

World War II

"Our pilot and co-pilot literally stood on the controls to right the plane for about a minute so the fellows could bail out," Suitts said.

Only five parachutes blossomed. Ellis and four other crewmen, three additional replacements for the Linz raid and navigator Arne Hansen, died with Tail Dragon. The crippled bomber slammed into the earth from twenty-three thousand feet up. Lieutenant Edwin "Pappy" Boyer, the pilot, and the four others who bailed out became prisoners of war.

"Herbert had shown me his rosary beads and St. Christopher's Medal," Suitts said. "He was sure he would make it. He always attended religious services before we went on a mission. We lost him on just his fifth mission."

In the spring and summer of 1944, Bob Suitts braved massed flak guns and swarms of Nazi fighter planes in bombing raids against enemy targets in nine German-occupied countries. He spent up to thirteen hours in the air on some missions.

"Munich, Germany, Vienna, Austria—we called it 'Flak Alley'—the oil refineries and storage facilities at Ploesti, Romania—they were some of the toughest," Suitts said.

Often, his planes limped home, shot full of holes. Spirit of '76 crash-landed and slid sixth-tenths of a mile on its belly before grinding to a halt. "The plane was completely wiped out," Suitts said. "We were shaken up, but thankfully none of us were hurt."

Suitts's flak wound came later. After World War II, he was promoted to first lieutenant and served in the Korean War as a nonflying maintenance officer. But the silver air gunner's wings, the Purple Heart and the three Air Medals pinned on his uniform marked him as a veteran combat flier in some of the bloodiest air battles in history.

Almost sixty-two thousand heavy bomber crewmen were killed, wounded or listed as missing in the European and Mediterranean Theaters in World War II. More than thirty-one thousand were taken prisoner. The 461st Bomb Group, part of the 15th Air Force, lost 108 planes and about six hundred men to enemy action in 1944–1945, Suitts said.

"We knew what we were up against but we were young and foolish, I guess, and didn't think about getting killed," Suitts said.

Suitts flew in B-24s from Toretta air field near sunbaked Cerignola, Italy. "Eight of us in the ten-man bomber crew I went overseas with got Purple Hearts," Suitts said. "Seven of us were wounded, including our tail gunner, who lost his arm, and Arne Hansen was killed."

Suitts didn't get a scratch until his fifteenth mission, May 24, 1944, when the 461st pounded a big German air base at Wiener Neustadt, Austria. Antiaircraft fire was heavy; twenty-three planes were hit, two shot down.

Flak found Suitts over Wiener Neustadt. A shell burst hurled a jagged, two-inch-long chunk of steel through the bomber's aluminum skin and into the nose gunner. "My right arm went limp. It felt like a hundred hornets were stinging my neck and shoulder."

Suitts spent a dozen days in the hospital and eight weeks more on the mend. "I was pretty heavily sedated in the hospital," he said. "Supposedly, I said I was going to wipe out the entire German air force for what they did to me. Of course, I couldn't do that in a bomber—that was for guys like 'Herky' Green."

Green's storied fighter group sometimes helped protect the 461st against German fighters. "You could see those checker-tail Mustangs coming from a long way off," Suitts said. "We were always glad to see them, especially 'Herky' Green's plane."

Suitts left the air force in 1957. He worked as a machinist in Dekalb County, Illinois, until 1994 when he and his wife, Helen, retired to Wingo, a tiny Graves County town near Mayfield.

Suitts hadn't thought about Herky Green in a long time. But when Suitts told a local real estate agent that he was a gunner in Italy-based U.S. bombers in World War II, she mentioned a monument at the courthouse in Mayfield.

"She said it was to this Mayfield man who was a fighter ace in the Mediterranean Theater in World War II. She didn't know his first name, but I said it must have been 'Herky.'"

Suitts climbed in his car and made a beeline for the Graves County courthouse. He found Green's memorial. "I never dreamed I'd end up living just eight miles from where he was born and raised," Suitts said with a grin.

"The Good Lord Surely Smiled on Us Today"

Tech Sergeant Bill Uvanni heard the awful "whoomph" of the exploding German antiaircraft shell.

Shrapnel slashed into his protective flak vest, ripping out cotton stuffing that fluttered around him like snow. He feared "flak had torn right through my…vest."

Uvanni was unhurt. But that flak burst high over Hamburg, Germany, on August 6, 1944, was apparently his nearest brush with death in World War II.

A radio operator on a B-24 Liberator bomber, Uvanni braved flak and enemy fighters on thirty-five combat missions. He chronicled every one.

World War II

"Maybe in my youth and in the excitement I saw things differently than others," he wrote. "However, in my heart it is as recorded in this diary."

A native of Rome, New York, Uvanni settled with his wife, Nell, in Paducah, her hometown, after the war. Bill Uvanni died in 1999 at age seventy-nine. His combat journal survives as grim testimony to some of the bloodiest air battles of World War II.

Until her death, Nell Uvanni treasured her husband's diary and the decorations for valor he earned in the skies over Nazi-ruled Europe. Uvanni won a Distinguished Flying Cross and a quartet of Air Medals.

"While he was overseas, he wrote about each mission after it happened," Nell Uvanni said. "It was all in a little book. When the war was over, he typed it up."

Bill Uvanni remembered two missions when he "was freezing and sweating at the same time." They were his first and last. "The temperature at high altitude was usually extremely cold and accounts for the freezing, but, it was tension that caused the sweating," he explained.

Uvanni had good reason to sweat. In World War II, German fighter pilots and antiaircraft gunners shot down 152 B-24s in his outfit, the storied Forty-fourth Bomb Group, dubbed the Flying 8 Balls. More than 850 air crewmen were killed.

"Bill and his crew were lucky," Nell Uvanni said. "They all got home except their navigator, who was shot down and killed when he had to fly with another crew."

Nell and Bill were married stateside before he joined the Forty-fourth Bomb Group at Shipdham, England, in 1944. Uvanni, then twenty-four, and nine other fliers crewed a B-24 they nicknamed Consolidated Mess.

Consolidated Aircraft Company made the B-24. "I guess 'Mess' was just for fun," Nell said with a grin.

There was no fun flying a bomber in combat. On Uvanni's first mission, a July 7, 1944 raid against Bernberg, Germany, about sixty cannon-firing German Messerschmitt 410 fighters pounced on the Forty-fourth.

"None of the planes from our squadron [was]…hit but an entire squadron (12 aircraft) [was]…knocked out on the first pass," he wrote. "Some blew up and others went into dives and never came out."

After several men from stricken B-24s managed to bail out, Consolidated Mess's radio crackled with frightening news. German pilots were shooting the Americans dangling helplessly in their parachutes. U.S. P-38 fighters, which were escorting the bombers, shot down many of the Messerschmitts—"really paid them off," according to Uvanni.

Consolidated Mess got home to Shipdham. "At interrogation the intelligence officer told us that missions didn't come any rougher than today's," Uvanni wrote.

There were many more rough ones. But Uvanni's B-24 was proving to be a survivor. "So far we've had no serious battle damage—the Mess seems rather charmed," he marveled after mission five.

But death claimed Uvanni's friend, Johnny Raniello, a flier who bunked next to him. Raniello was a radio operator on another B-24.

On July 29, 1944, the group was on a raid against Bremen, Germany, when Raniello's plane collided with another B-24. Both bombers crashed into the English Channel; only one man lived. "[Raniello] had a picture of his baby he had never seen tacked to the ceiling over his bed so he could look at it as he lay on his bunk," Uvanni wrote.

Eight days later, Consolidated Mess was again bound for Germany with a load of bombs. The Flying 8 Balls knew the target was a rough one: a Nazi oil refinery at Hamburg.

A storm of antiaircraft fire greeted the Americans. "We could see planes going down ahead of us as they entered the barrage," Uvanni wrote. "It looked impossible for an airplane to get through."

As Consolidated Mess neared the target, Uvanni opened the bomb bay doors and sat on the floor behind the pilot and copilot.

> *When the bombs dropped, I jumped to close the bomb bay doors (not that it would protect us, but it sure helps morale!)*
>
> *I had no sooner closed the doors and turned around than "WHOOMPH" a burst of flak hit us and right where I was sitting, a hole the size of a 50 cent piece appeared! My flak vest was covered with cotton batting and the air was filled with it—I thought at first that I had been hit.*

Uvanni and the rest of the crew were unscathed, although shrapnel lacerated Consolidated Mess from nose to tail. Like Uvanni, the tail gunner had a close call when shrapnel "ripped through the fuselage right in front of…[him], missed his head by inches and tore through some K-rations he stored. They were torn to pieces!!"

So was a B-24 flying behind Consolidated Mess. Another flak burst blew off the plane's right wing. "It started down in a crazy spin and no chutes came out. We watched it all the way down and it landed in a small town and blew up. It must have had its bombs [be]cause the explosion seemed to cover the whole town."

World War II

Consolidated Mess got its crew home safely yet again. The B-24 "had holes in the left wing a foot long; holes in the flight deck; in the bomb bays; in the tail section; holes beneath the pilot and co-pilot seats and holes in the nose compartment and not one of our crew had received a scratch!!!" Uvanni wrote. "The Good Lord surely smiled on us today."

"A Heroic Example of Courage and Fortitude"

Private First Class Luther Skaggs Jr., U.S. Marine Corps, hoped the night was dark enough—and his foxhole deep enough—to hide him from the Japanese.

But an enemy hand grenade plopped beside him and exploded. The blast mangled his left leg.

The pain was searing. He refused to summon a corpsman, lest he reveal his outfit's position.

So the twenty-one-year-old Kentuckian his buddies called "a tough little guy" wrapped a tourniquet around his bloody, shrapnel-shredded limb. He

Skaggs's tombstone. *Courtesy of the author.*

stayed put for eight more hours, shooting his rifle and tossing grenades at the Japanese.

Skaggs's heroism gained him the Medal of Honor and promotion to corporal. But it cost him the lower part of his leg.

He was still on crutches from the amputation when President Harry S. Truman fastened the medal and its starry, sky-blue ribbon around his neck at the White House in July 1945.

Skaggs succumbed to lung cancer on April 4, 1976, at age fifty-three. He was buried in Arlington National Cemetery but was not forgotten in his native Henderson County.

Born and reared in the Geneva community, Skaggs joined the marines in 1942. Two years later, he landed on Guam with the Third Battalion of the Third Marine Division on Guam.

Skaggs was a squad leader with a mortar section of a rifle company, according to his Medal of Honor Citation, which President Franklin D. Roosevelt signed. He won his country's highest decoration for valor on the night of July 21–22, 1944.

"When the section leader became a casualty under a heavy mortar barrage shortly after landing, Private First Class Skaggs promptly assumed command and led the section through intense fire for a distance of 200 yards to a position from which to deliver effective coverage of the assault on a strategic cliff," the citation explained.

> *Valiantly defending this vital position against strong enemy counterattacks during the night, Private First Class Skaggs was critically wounded when a Japanese grenade lodged in his foxhole and exploded, shattering the lower part of one leg. Quick to act, he applied an improvised tourniquet and, while propped up in his foxhole, gallantly returned the enemy's fire with his rifle and hand grenades for a period of eight hours, later crawling unassisted to the rear to continue to fight until the Japanese had been annihilated. Uncomplaining and calm throughout this critical period, Private First Class Skaggs served as a heroic example of courage and fortitude to other wounded men and, by his courageous leadership and inspiring devotion to duty, upheld the highest traditions for the United States Naval Service.*

The Japanese fought hard for Guam, the largest of the Mariana Islands. Almost six thousand Japanese troops had wrested the island from fewer than six hundred U.S. marines and sailors in December 1941.

The Americans were determined to retake Guam.

World War II

Skaggs was part of a thirty-six-thousand-man assault force of marines and soldiers that stormed ashore on July 21. The island's twenty-two thousand defenders fought tenaciously.

Guam did not fall to the Americans until August 8. Fighting had been savage; 7,800 marines and soldiers were killed or wounded. Fewer than 3,000 Japanese survived; many of the enemy perished in suicide charges.

A year after he sacrificed his limb and almost lost his life, Skaggs was welcomed back to Henderson, the Henderson County seat. The town declared his homecoming Luther Skaggs Day.

"It was a great day," reporter Tom Taylor quoted Lewis N. Johnson in an April 8, 1976 *Henderson Gleaner* story about Skaggs when he died. "The parade that day was probably the most elaborate that this city has ever seen. Patriotism was high at that time and the turnout to greet Skaggs was tremendous."

Taylor also wrote that Skaggs proudly wore his Medal of Honor. "Johnson and another Hendersonian, Charles D. Mulligan, both decorated veterans who were wounded in action, shared the speakers' platform with Skaggs," he added.

Harold Dodson, who helped organize Luther Skaggs Day, told the *Gleaner* how the idea started:

> *As soon as Luther was presented the award by the President, we received a picture of the ceremony here at home. The moment we saw that photograph, we decided that Henderson would do something to honor him on his homecoming.*
>
> *All the civic and fraternal organizations in the city pitched in to make the event a success. The military at Ft. Knox sent down all sorts of equipment, tanks, jeeps and personnel carriers, for the parade which was probably the biggest ever in Henderson.*
>
> *The carpenters union built a speakers' platform in front of the courthouse for free and the newspaper gave a lot of help. You wouldn't have believed the crowd that turned out.*

Taylor wrote, "Virtually every photograph of the events of that day shows Skaggs with an ear-to-ear grin, despite the crutches and pinned-up pantleg, life-long reminders of the eight-hour ordeal which earned him the nation's respect."

After he was discharged from the marines in 1946, Skaggs stayed in Washington, working as a budget analyst in the Defense Department and later as a Veterans Administration (VA) employee until his retirement, according to the *Gleaner*.

"In 1961 he became the first enlisted man to head the Congressional Medal of Honor Society, an honor he shared with three generals," Taylor wrote. "He was elected in Washington during the inauguration of President John F. Kennedy."

Skaggs's life ended in Sarasota, Florida, where he moved after he left the VA. "All those who knew Luther Skaggs were stunned and saddened to learn…of his death," an April 9, 1976 *Gleaner* story said.

The article explained that "Skaggs lost a portion of his left leg in service to his country. But those who knew him best will tell you that he never lost the courage and fortitude which carried him through the fighting on Guam."

The article concluded that Skaggs's burial, "with full military rites," was "a nation's way of honoring a man in death who, in life, brought so much honor to himself, his family, his community and his country."

"Look Out, Shipley!"

Private First Class Richard Shipley, USMC, did not see the Japanese hand grenade that flew from the darkness and landed in the foxhole he was sharing with Private First Class Wesley Phelps of Ohio County.

Phelps did. "Look out, Shipley!" he yelled. Then Phelps fell on the grenade. It exploded, slightly wounding Shipley. The blast killed Phelps, who was born in Neafus, a tiny Grayson County community, but grew up in Rosine, a small town in Ohio County.

Phelps's sacrifice in the bloody Battle of Peleliu earned him the Medal of Honor.

"Courageous and indomitable, Private First Class Phelps fearlessly gave his life that another might be spared serious injury and his great valor and heroic devotion to duty in the face of certain death reflected the highest credit upon himself and the United States Naval Service," his Medal of Honor citation reads. "He gallantly gave his life for his country."

Phelps is buried in the cemetery at Rosine. A six-foot stone, topped by a bronze eagle, marks his grave, which is near the final resting place of country music star Bill Monroe, a Rosine native.

A state historical marker on U.S. Highway 62 in Rosine also commemorates Phelps's heroism halfway around the world from his native western Kentucky. Phelps probably had never heard of Peleliu when he was drafted in the marines in 1943.

World War II

Phelps's tombstone.
Courtesy of the author.

He was twenty-one when he landed at Peleliu with the First Marine Division on September 15, 1944. Japanese resistance was ferocious.

Phelps was a light machine gun crewman in Company K, Third Battalion, Seventh Regiment, of the division. Company K advanced toward the top of one of the steep ridges that form the backbone of Peleliu.

Phelps's citation explains that, after dark on October 4, the Japanese launched "a savage hostile counterattack," hurling grenades at the marines, who had dug foxholes into the hillside. "Stationed with another Marine in an advanced position when a Japanese hand grenade landed in his foxhole, Private First Class Phelps instantly shouted a warning to his comrade and rolled over on the deadly bomb, absorbing with his own Body the full, shattering impact of the exploding charge," the citation says.

Not until November 27 did the Battle for Peleliu end in American victory. About 17,500 marines and 11,000 soldiers from the Army Eighty-first Infantry Division assaulted the island, which was defended by about 11,000 Japanese.

Almost 1,800 Americans were killed and more than 8,000 were wounded. All but about 200 Japanese were killed.

Phelps was buried in Peleliu, but his remains were reinterred in the Rosine cemetery later in 1944. Thirty-six years afterward, the citizens of Rosine decided Phelps merited more than a "modest tombstone," Stewart Jennison wrote in the *Owensboro Messenger-Inquirer* on May 26, 1980, Memorial Day. They wanted it replaced "with something that showed their pride in Ohio County's most decorated warrior," he added.

The monument was unveiled on May 25. "Ada Belle Sikes, the only surviving member of Phelps' immediate family, was led forward to remove the crimson wrap which covered the six-foot monument," according to Jennison. "A full colorguard and 21-gun salute gave the occasion a somber significance that caused even the youngest children to lower their heads."

Jennison quoted John Blackburn, a local historian: "A soldier who gave his life is honored here. But as he is honored, so are we. This young man was one of us.—a fellow American, a fellow Ohio Countian."

Blackburn added:

> *There are standards of conduct that our military men and women are expected to meet. The American people have never been willing to compromise for less that these strict and lofty rules. Those who do not go beyond this call need not feel they have failed in service…But there are some who respond by going beyond, who risk their lives in a display of outstanding gallantry and bravery, only these can receive the highest honor this nation can bestow.*

Sikes, who lived in Roseville, was Phelps's sister. After a wreath was laid on the new monument, Rosine citizens comforted her, Jennison wrote. "The memory of losing a brother 36 years ago was harshly rekindled only Friday when her remaining brother, Lee died. Today, Mrs. Sikes must return to the Rosine cemetery for his burial."

Sikes recalled the telegram that came, telling the family about their loved one's death. She remembered a letter from Shipley, which told Phelps's heroism, Jennison wrote.

Before the telegram, the family had only received "cheerful letters," according to Sikes. She told Jennison her brother's letters promised, "There's nothing to worry about. I'm coming home."

World War II

"I Didn't Have Any Time for Sightseeing"

Elevators whisk tourists to the top of Paris's Eiffel Tower in minutes.

Louis Chappell's trip took about an hour. He hoofed it up the stairs, lugging a thirty-pound pack in an icy December breeze.

"It was a little scary, and I was tired," the Paducah veteran remembered. "But we had a job to do."

On December 17, 1944, Army sergeant Louis Chappell helped rig a radio transmitter atop the 1,063-foot tower in the French capital to warn away Allied warplanes. "The city was still blacked out at night then," said Chappell, who came home from World War II with a Bronze Star medal.

In 1993, Chappell returned to Paris, where Gustav Eiffel's steel tower is probably the City of Light's most famous landmark. "I went up again, and the city looked pretty much the same to me," he said.

Chappell's mission wasn't a headline grabber like the Allied invasion of Normandy six months before. But it did earn a paragraph in *Stars and Stripes*, the military newspaper, and rated a sentence in an official army history book.

Chappell isn't mentioned. "Still, it's still nice to see what you did in the history books," he said.

The tower, which has attracted tourists, lovers, protesters, moviemakers and suicides, had elevators in 1944. They just didn't work on December 17. "They were powered hydraulically and were all frozen up," Chappell said.

There are 1,665 steps leading to the top, according to the official Eiffel Tower website. "Every time we stopped to rest, I took a knife and carved my initials and the date into the paint," Chappell said.

Chappell said heights did not particularly bother him. "But there was ice all over, and water was dripping down from a leaky toilet."

Most tourists enjoy the view from atop the tower. "But I didn't have any time for sightseeing," Chappell said. "I was too busy."

Chappell went up the tower with a lieutenant from his unit, the 3372nd Signal Service Battalion, Army Signal Corps. "There were about eight hundred soldiers in our outfit," he said. "It was an honor to get to go."

Chappell and the officer hooked up a British-made air navigation warning device called a "squeaker." The contraption made a noise that could be heard on British and American airplane radios.

Stars and Stripes reported Chappell's mission under the headline "U.S. Gets Eiffel Tower." The two-sentence story explained: "The Eiffel Tower is an item of France's reverse lend-lease to the U.S. It has been requisitioned by the Air Forces for use as a radio station."

The Signal Corps: The Outcome (Mid-1943 through 1945), part of the *U.S. Army in World War II* history series, only noted that "A British No. 10 (a 6-centimeter pulse set) was installed in the Eiffel Tower in Paris."

"I Don't Know What Was Worse, the Cold or the Germans"

Corporal Hargus Haywood of the 101st Airborne Division had no idea where he was going when he got orders to move out from Mourmelon, France, on December 18, 1944.

"They loaded us into open trailer trucks and drove us all night," the Mayfield man said. En route, rain turned to snow.

"It was almost daylight when we reached this town. I still didn't know where we were, but we started receiving a lot of artillery fire. The next day, the Germans surrounded us."

Darkness had hidden red, yellow and black signs at the city limits. Bullet nicked, one of the signs is in the Pratt Museum at Fort Campbell, home of the famed 101st Airborne Division (Air Assault), which now fights from helicopters.

"Bastogne," it reads.

Haywood retired from the old Continental-General Tire plant near Mayfield. He was a storeroom clerk and member of United Steelworkers Local 665.

In December 1944, Haywood was among twelve thousand paratroopers who had arrived smack in the middle of the Battle of the Bulge, the biggest battle the U.S. Army ever fought. The 101st Airborne troopers dubbed the fight their "rendezvous with destiny."

Haywood said the Americans faced twin foes. "I don't know what was worse, the cold or the Germans," he said.

A native of Floyd County in eastern Kentucky, Haywood lied about his age and enlisted in the army in 1940 when he was sixteen. "I'd never been farther from home than Lexington," he remembered.

A coal miner's son, Haywood said he volunteered for the paratroopers "because I wanted some excitement." His wife, Evelyn, remembers it differently. "It was that extra fifty-dollars-a-month jump pay," she said, laughing.

Haywood had just turned twenty-one when 101st Airborne troopers, dubbed the Screaming Eagles, found themselves in harm's way at lightly defended Bastogne, Belgium. The division was dispatched to help save the market town that straddled the path of a German juggernaut, which seemed unstoppable. "We knew we had to hold on," Haywood said. "We knew we had to fight to the death."

Early on December 16, 250,000 German troops and one thousand Nazi tanks sprang a surprise attack out of the snowy woods. Before the 101st Airborne and other reinforcements arrived, only about 75,000 Americans stood between the Nazis and victory.

Supported by artillery and advancing on a sixty-mile front, the enemy shoved a deep bulge (hence the name of the battle) in American lines around Bastogne, which the Germans encircled on December 20. They expected to wipe out the Americans quickly or force them to give up.

Thick fog helped hide the Nazis and prevented U.S. and British warplanes from bombing and strafing the enemy columns. "It was so foggy we couldn't fire our howitzers," Haywood said. "We couldn't see anything to shoot at."

A combat medic with the 463rd Parachute Field Artillery Battalion, he had earned his baptism of fire as part of an Allied airborne task force that parachuted into German-held Sicily in 1943. He jumped with the 82nd Airborne Division.

Day and night, the Nazis pounded beleaguered Bastogne with long-range artillery. The shell-blasted snow was stained with the blood of dead and wounded GIs. Frostbite was a danger, too, in the bitter cold.

"About all we had for the wounded were small vials of morphine, some aspirin tablets and bandages," Haywood said. "A lot of guys died before we could get them to a field hospital."

Haywood recalled Private Howard Hickenlooper of the 463rd. A German rifle bullet pierced his neck. "He was a short guy, with kind of a ruddy complexion. About all I could do was comfort him.

"He didn't make it. His wife had just had twins, too. He never knew it. She told him in a letter that arrived later."

Haywood's thoughts were on his wife and their fifteen-month-old son, Ronie, back in Buchanan, Tennessee, Evelyn's hometown. "I was afraid I'd never see them again, but I tried to keep my spirits up by talking with the guys about baseball and basketball. I was a big Cincinnati Reds and Kentucky Wildcats fan, even then."

Foxhole conversations often were interrupted by exploding German shells or by the rumble of Nazi tanks churning through six-inch-deep snow. "They got pretty close, too, those tanks. You could see the SS troopers coming in their white snow suits," said Haywood, who added that some 463rd gunners managed to destroy a few German tanks by using their little 75 mm pack howitzers as antitank guns.

On December 22, a delegation of German officers, waving a white flag, came over to the Americans and told them to surrender or be annihilated. Brigadier General Anthony McAuliffe of the 101st refused with the famous reply, "Nuts."

When the Germans, who spoke English, asked an American officer to explain what McAuliffe meant, the officer replied, "In plain English it is the same as 'Go to hell,'" according to *Bastogne: The First Eight Days* by S.L.A. Marshall. The officer added: "If you continue to attack we will kill every goddamn German that tries to break into this city."

On December 26, tanks of the Fourth Armored Division smashed through the Germans to relieve Bastogne and its battle-weary defenders, which included other soldiers besides the paratroopers. "It was the happiest day of my life," Haywood said. "We couldn't thank those tankers enough."

After the war, Haywood discovered that one of his Fourth Armored Division liberators was his brother-in-law, Brent Morris of Murray. He drove a Sherman tank into Bastogne.

Private First Class Gardner Seay of Mayfield rode into Bastogne aboard a Fourth Armored Division halftrack. "Those paratroopers were afraid we were Germans at first," Seay said. "The Germans had gotten some American uniforms."

By January 1945, the bulge had been erased, and the massive Anglo-American offensive against Germany resumed. Squeezed by American and British forces attacking from the west and by Soviet armies advancing from the east, Germany surrendered on May 7, 1945. The Allies officially claimed victory on May 8, V-E Day.

Haywood, who made staff sergeant, kept his olive green army dress uniform. His silver jump wings are fastened above the left breast pocket. Multicolored battle ribbons are rowed up below.

A special blue ribbon, framed in gold, is pinned over the right breast pocket. "That's a Presidential Unit Citation we got for Bastogne," he said.

Famous Journalist Got Paducah War Hero's Name Wrong

First Lieutenant Frank Kolb and his infantry company went down in history as the first U.S. troops "to set foot on German ground" in World War II.

The western Kentuckian never claimed credit for the feat. "It was a good day anyway," he said in a 1999 interview. "I didn't lose anybody."

World War II

Kolb. *Courtesy of Susan Phipps.*

Kolb died in 2000 at age seventy-seven. He was retired from his family's business, Kolb Brothers Drug Company in Paducah.

A Paducah native who lived in Mayfield after the war, Kolb earned four Silver Stars, a Bronze Star and a Purple Heart in seven campaigns with the First Infantry Division. He might have been the youngest company commander in the storied Big Red One.

Kolb was twenty-one when he fought his way through the Siegfried Line, Adolf Hitler's vaunted defense barrier, and trod German soil near Aachen. The date was September 13, 1944. Kolb made headlines in the *Stars and Stripes*. "The story also got in the *New York Times* and a lot of other papers," he said.

Kolb got in a history book, too. "Kolb's men were the first American soldiers to set foot on German ground," wrote Irving Werstein in *The Battle of Aachen*. "At least my name was spelled right in the book," Kolb said, grinning. "It was wrong in all of the papers."

After Kolb and his men breached the Siegfried Line, a *Stars and Stripes* reporter interviewed the young lieutenant. He got the story right, but not Kolb's name.

"After ten years of talk about the Siegfried Line, 21-year-old 1/Lt. Bob Kalb, of Paducah, Ky., took his company through it without a casualty," the reporter wrote. "Since Kalb and his men forced the first opening, the armored unit working with this crack infantry division has been pouring through the gap." Lieutenant "Kalb" told the reporter, "We knocked out about 15 or 20 pillboxes, I guess."

Kolb kept a clipping of the *Stars and Stripes* story. The reporter is still a journalist, but on national network TV.

He is Andy Rooney of CBS's *60 Minutes*.

Kolb said other First Infantry soldiers may have beaten his outfit into Germany. Some Third Armored Division tank crews claimed they were the first, Kolb remembered.

"What does it matter who was first?" Kolb asked. "I didn't think it was that important then. I still don't."

By September 1944, Kolb was already a battle-hardened veteran. The Germans captured him in combat in North Africa, but he escaped.

He fought through Sicily. He landed on Omaha Beach on D-Day and then fought across France to the German border, guarded by what the enemy called the Westwall. The Allies nicknamed it the Siegfried Line.

Three miles deep on average, the concrete and barbed wire bulwark bristled with "hundreds of mutually-supporting pillboxes, troop shelters and command posts," wrote MacDonald in his book *The Mighty Endeavor*. "Where no natural antitank obstacle existed, German engineers had constructed pyramidical concrete projections called 'dragon's teeth,' draped in parallel rows across hills and valleys like some scaly-backed reptile."

Similarly, Rooney described the wide defense belt as

> *a series of strategically-placed pillboxes. In the hilly country of the border, roads run through the valley, and the Germans placed the fortified concrete igloos in positions which commanded the only possible entry for vehicles. On both sides of the roads, concrete "dragon's teeth" extended for miles, preventing tanks from rolling over the open country between the road networks.*

When Kolb and his troops attacked on the morning of September 13, 1944, they were out front in "a general offensive along every mile of the Westwall from Holland to Switzerland," Werstein wrote. Kolb and his men ducked and dodged through the dragon's teeth, meeting unexpectedly light enemy resistance. "The line would have been tough to crack if the Germans had had enough men to man it the way it should have been," Kolb suggested to Rooney.

World War II

Even so, Kolb knew he needed armor to knock out the German "igloos." A platoon of tank destroyers—Sherman tanklike vehicles with open-top turrets and powerful guns—got the job done.

"Our…[tank destroyer] fired at some of them from about 20 yards and blasted them wide open," Rooney quoted Kolb. "They'd roll right up and fire a ninety millimeter shell through the aperture," Kolb recalled fifty-five years later. "The back door would fly open, and the Germans would come running out. They found a woman with one group, a good-looking blonde."

Sometimes, Kolb said in 1999, the Germans surrendered as soon as a thirty-one-ton tank destroyer pointed its long-barreled gun at their pillbox. "The ordinary German soldier had enough sense to give up when he knew he was beaten."

After a while, the rest of Kolb's battalion passed through his company. He remembered talking to Don Whitehead of the Associated Press, another famous war correspondent, in a break from battle. "I was just glad none of my men had been killed. I don't think any of them had even been wounded."

"Skippy" Skinner, Kolb's buddy from Paducah, wasn't so lucky. By chance, Kolb spotted him in another company that moved ahead of his outfit.

"I told Skippy, 'Don't forget to duck,'" Kolb said. He added that a German tank shell killed Skinner hours later.

Werstein said that by punching through the Siegfried Line and capturing Aachen, the Americans won a great victory, "a harbinger of what was to befall the [German] nation whose people and leaders had dreamed of ruling the world." But an infantry soldier doesn't always know when a battle is won, said Kolb, who made captain before he turned twenty-two. He fought in the Huertgen Forest, the Battle of the Bulge and other bloody combat battles before the Nazi surrender took effect on May 8, 1945.

"My little walkie-talkie could pick up the BBC [British Broadcasting Corporation] if I was up high enough," he said. "I remember climbing up on this hill in Sicily and hearing all about 'the victorious American army.' We'd had the hell beaten out of us that day and hadn't gained a thing."

Booze, Not Bubbly, Launched Cargo Ship Named for the Nelson County Seat

Officials skipped the champagne when they christened the SS *Bardstown Victory* in World War II.

"They used bourbon from Bardstown," said Dixie Hibbs, a Bardstown historian and author.

She suspects the *Bardstown Victory*, which carried troops and cargo, might be the only vessel ever launched with a bottle of booze. "But it was appropriate," she said. "Bardstown is synonymous with bourbon. When you walk other places, you stop and sell the roses. In Bardstown, you smell the mash."

Hibbs said at least a half dozen distilleries were operating in the Nelson County seat on February 15, 1945, when the late Emily Carothers christened the *Bardstown Victory* at the Bethlehem-Fairfield Shipyard in Baltimore. The ceremony grabbed headlines in the *Bardstown Standard*.

"A number of former Bardstown people and other Kentuckians" watched as she broke the booze bottle over the *Bardstown Victory*'s steel bow, the paper said. "The use of bourbon for the christening set a precedent for ship christenings." Others in the ceremony included H.S. Atchison, a Kentucky native who was general manager of the Baltimore branch of the Standard Oil Company, the *Standard* said. Carothers's work earned her "a large bouquet of roses," according to the paper.

The *Bardstown Victory* was the thirty-third Victory Ship launched for merchant marine service. It was the fifth christened in February 1945. "The keel was laid December 4, 1944, and 73 days were required for construction," the *Standard* reported.

The paper said Carothers was "a descendant of old and prominent families in Bardstown." She was chosen to christen the *Bardstown Victory* "by popular vote of the citizens of Bardstown."

How the ceremonial bourbon was selected is unclear. City officials did not want to play favorites among the whiskey makers.

Supposedly, each distillery submitted a bottle. "Somewhere between Kentucky and the bow of the ship, a little of each one was poured into one bottle," Hibbs said. "This might have been a way to truthfully assure each distiller, 'Your whiskey was the one used to christen the ship.'"

The bottle was wrapped in red, white and blue ribbon, which Carothers reportedly brought home as a souvenir.

After the war, the *Bardstown Victory* ferried U.S. troops home from Europe. "Ten months after it was christened, William Paul Berry of New Haven was one of 1,897 soldiers it brought back," Hibbs said.

A trio of World War II Liberty Ships—cargo and troop carriers like the Victory Ships—bore Nelson County names: the SS *Marie Mattingly Meloney*, *Charles A. Wickliffe* and the *J.C.W. Beckham*. "Meloney grew up in Bardstown, left and became a famous journalist," Hibbs said. Wickliffe was a Kentucky governor; Beckham was a lieutenant governor and governor.

World War II

"How Can I Be Sore at Him? My Father Fought under that Flag!"

The highest-ranking American soldier killed in battle in World War II was a Kentuckian. Even so, Lieutenant General Simon Bolivar Buckner Jr. is still overshadowed by his father.

"Literally," Trowbridge said. "His mom and dad are buried under full-length gravestones in the Frankfort Cemetery. Just below them on the hillside, shorter, smaller footstones mark the graves of junior and his wife."

Simon Bolivar Buckner Sr. was a Confederate lieutenant general. He was also governor of Kentucky from 1887 to 1891.

Buckner Jr. also earned three stars, but in the U.S. Army. He died in the 1945 Battle of Okinawa.

Okinawa was the bloodiest fight in the Pacific Theater. An unexpected Japanese artillery barrage killed Buckner. He was fifty-eight.

The general was one of about 12,500 Americans who lost their lives on Okinawa. About 100,000 Japanese soldiers died in the battle or committed suicide. In addition, as many as 150,000 civilians perished in the deadly crossfire between the two armies.

"The general was smiling when hit and it remained on his face in death," an Associated Press wire story quoted Buckner's aide. The general's Tenth Army fought on "toward imminent, final victory to avenge the death of its commander on the field of battle," another AP story said.

Buckner was born in 1886, twenty-one years after the end of his father's war. He came into the world at Glen Lily, the family's antebellum home near Munfordville, the Hart County seat. Buckner "had been born" to lead the invasion of Okinawa, *Time* magazine claimed.

"The youngster grew up in a rugged, outdoor life, its setting the lovely, wooded country of rolling hills known in Kentucky as the 'Pennyr'y'l,'" the article said. Headlined "Buck's Battle," *Time* ran the piece on April 16, 1945, two weeks and two days after the first Americans scrambled out of their landing crafts onto Okinawa, just four hundred miles from Japan.

"'I went barefooted," *Time* quoted from Buckner's writing, "hunted, trapped, fished, swam, canoed, raised chickens, fought roosters, rode five miles daily for the mail, trained dogs, did odd farm jobs, learned not to eat green persimmons and occasionally walked eight miles to Munfordville to broaden my horizon by seeing the train come in, learning the fine points of horse trading or listening to learned legal and political discussion on County Court Day.'"

He enrolled at Virginia Military Institute in 1902. Two years later, President Theodore Roosevelt, the late governor Buckner's friend, appointed the young Kentuckian to the U.S. Military Academy at West Point, wrote Lloyd J. Graybar in "The Buckners of Kentucky," an article published in the *Filson Club History Quarterly* in 1984.

Buckner graduated in 1908 and was commissioned an infantry lieutenant. He was disappointed to miss combat in World War I but was perhaps glad to return to his alma mater in 1933 as commandant of cadets.

He stayed three years. "In this post, Buckner added to his reputation as a stern disciplinarian," Graybar wrote. "At West Point's summer camp, he ordered all cold cream and after-shave lotion confiscated, saying 'Cadets should work and smell like men.'"

Buckner was dubbed "Bull" because of his "commanding personality and for his massive, weatherbeaten appearance and propensity to use the full power of his lungs when he felt necessary," according to Graybar. "His treatment of the cadets had already prompted one parent to make the now legendary complaint: 'Buckner forgets that cadets are born, not quarried.'"

Buckner was back commanding full-fledged soldiers at the onset of World War II. The army had put him in charge of Alaska's defenses, which were tested in 1942 when Japanese forces seized tiny Attu and Kiska, among the westernmost of the far-flung Aleutian Islands.

The enemy left in 1943, the year Buckner was promoted to lieutenant general. "Buckner would have liked to use Alaska as a base for advance on Japan via the Aleutians and proposed the toast, 'May you walk in the ashes of Tokyo' with his favorite beverage—bourbon of course," Graybar added. "But the severe climate conditions led strategic planners to reject a northern advance."

Buckner stayed in Alaska after the Japanese gave up Attu and Kiska. But all was not quiet on the northern front. Buckner almost got fired for claiming Admiral Robert Theobald, his navy counterpart, was too timid to pursue the enemy. Buckner satirized Theobald in verse, which Graybar quoted:

> *The Bering Sea is not for me nor for my Fleet Headquarters.*
> *In noted dread I look ahead in wild Aleutian waters*
> *Where hidden reefs and willawaws and terrifying critters*
> *Unnerve me quite with woeful fright and give me fits and jitters.*

General George C. Marshall, the army chief of staff, was not happy to receive copies of the poem. Naturally, he was determined to minimize interservice rivalry, Graybar wrote.

World War II

But even Theobald conceded Buckner should not be relieved over the doggerel. In the end, the navy relieved Theobald, who was evidently as irascible as Buckner was.

Buckner fared better than his rival; he was promoted to lieutenant general in 1943 and, the next year, merited a transfer to warmer climes. He was Hawaii bound.

Better yet, the transfer included command of the newly formed Tenth Army. "For Buckner it would mean the combat he had long desired," Graybar wrote. "But when he took charge, the new army had neither a mission nor combat troops."

In 1945, he got a mission and the troops to carry it out. Buckner's soldiers would combine with the Marine III Amphibious Corps, led by Lieutenant General Roy Geiger, in an air-land-sea attack on strategic Okinawa in the Ryukus Islands, just four hundred miles from Japan. Thus, Buckner would get a crack at the enemy homeland but via a southerly route.

Buckner and Geiger sent their 183,000 men ashore on April 1. The *Time* reporter described Buckner as "a ruddy-faced, white-thatched, driving apostle of the vigorous life. Commands flowed from him in his normal conversational tones—roars, shouts and bellows. His celebrated laugh rolled out. Said one who had heard it: 'It starts with a little chuckle in his throat and then he really lets go and shakes the walls.'"

The Americans landed with deceptive ease, quickly advancing inland from their beachheads. The attackers did not know that the island's more than 100,000 Japanese defenders were waiting in caves and man-made strongholds away from the coast.

"Ground operations soon became exceedingly difficult as the well-sited Japanese defenses began to be encountered," Graybar wrote. "The supporting ships were being hit hard by kamikaze attacks."

As a result, Nimitz, overall commander of the invasion, began complaining about the slow going ashore. The admiral and General Archer Vandergrift, the marine corps commandant, hastened to Okinawa to investigate.

"Within hours after his arrival, Nimitz witnessed one kamikaze attack and a conventional air raid as well," Graybar explained. "Not surprisingly he told Buckner in a conference held the next day, April 23, that ground operations should be accelerated so that the supporting fleet could be released for other tasks."

Okinawa was a ground operation, Buckner chided. The general's implication was "that the navy should keep 'its opinions to itself,'" Graybar wrote.

Nimitz's retort was icy, according to Graybar: "Yes, but ground though it may be, I'm losing a ship and a half a day. So if this line isn't moving within five days, we'll get someone here to move it so we can all get out from under these stupid air attacks."

The press jumped Buckner. The *New York Herald Tribune* lambasted the general's "ultra conservative" tactics. Columnist David Lawrence said the marines should have been unleashed to conduct their "type of campaign." In other words, hit the enemy hard and fast. Lawrence claimed "Okinawa was a 'worse example of military incompetence than Pearl Harbor,'" according to Graybar.

"All the ingredients for a bitter interservice wrangle were present at a moment when the army and navy would have to cooperate for the invasion of Japan, barely six months away according to plans," Graybar wrote. But Nimitz defended Buckner, calling the Okinawa campaign "a magnificent performance." He added that "Buckner's frontal tactics were best for the conditions on Okinawa. Secretary of the Navy James Forrestal and Admirals Richmond K. Turner and Marc Mitscher were already in Buckner's corner.

"The controversy abated, thanks in part to Nimitz's prestige," Graybar wrote. "By this time it was also evident to knowledgeable observers that decisive progress on the ground was indeed being made."

An all-out American assault cracked the Shuri Line—the main Japanese defense position—on May 14. "Two weeks later marines captured Shuri Castle, and it became clear that the end of the campaign was in sight," Graybar wrote.

Captain Julius Dusenberg's A Company, Red Battalion of the Fifth Marine Regiment, grabbed the enemy strongpoint. That accomplished, he unfurled a replica of the flag under which Simon Bolivar Buckner Sr. fought, according to an article by navy lieutenant commander Joe D. Haines in a 1986 issue of the *Okinawa Marine*.

Haines's story was posted on the U.S. Militaria Forum website. "The castle lay within the zone of the [army] 77th Infantry Division, known as the Statue of Liberty Boys," Haines explained. A Japanese rear guard had stalled the soldiers' advance.

On the other hand, Dusenberg's marines were poised to bag the fortress. Anxious to see his men win the prize, Marine Major General Pedro del Valle ordered the captain to "take that damned place if you can. I'll make the explanations." Dusenberg was happy to oblige, Haines wrote.

Once it was mission accomplished for the marines, Dusenberg removed his helmet and took out "a flag he had been carrying for just such a special occasion," Haines explained. "He raised the flag at the highest point of the castle and let loose with a rebel yell. The flag waving overhead was not the Stars and Stripes, but the Confederate Stars and Bars.

"Most of the Marines joined in the yell, but a disapproving New Englander supposedly remarked, 'What does he want now? Should we sing 'Dixie'?'"

Major General Andrew Bruce, the Seventy-seventh Division commander, was not amused. He protested to Bucker that the marines had stolen his thunder.

"But Buckner only mildly chided General del Valle, saying, "How can I be sore at him? My father fought under that flag!" Haines wrote. "Dusenberg's flag was presented to Gen. Buckner as a souvenir. Gen. Buckner remarked, "OK! Now, let's get on with the war!"

Buckner did not live to see victory, which came on June 21. On June 18, he headed to the forward observation post of the Third Battalion, Eighth Marine Regiment. He was killed about two hours after he arrived, according to the AP. "He was standing with other officers in a slight disk-like impression on the forward slope of the ridge, south of Kunishi Ridge," the story said.

The AP also reported that the general "had just been pointing out interesting bits of action to accompanying officers—tanks spurting flames into cave positions; civilians leaving caves to surrender and sharp fighting on an adjoining hillside—when the first shell exploded in the observation post and a fragment entered his left breast." The story added another quote from the general's aide: "They had been taking their own bloody time getting the range for when they fired they dropped six or seven around there all of a sudden."

Buckner was sitting on a rock when the shell fragment struck him. "After the shelling, Japanese snipers came out…Del Valle said that the observation post was very close behind the front line and the Kunishi Ridge was still being cleaned up. He dropped 1,200 casualties in taking the ridge with his First Marine Division."

Buckner was the only shellfire casualty. But the aide said, "I and a couple of other officers might have been scratched." The aide added that Buckner was alive but unconscious when he reached his side. "He didn't know what hit him," the aide said.

"The day before his death Buckner had expressed satisfaction that his forces had killed about 80,000 Japanese," the story said. "On that day, 1,549 Japanese were killed on Okinawa to 47 Americans—a ratio of 33 to 1."

Upon Buckner's death, Geiger took command of U.S. troops and finished off the Japanese. Shortly before he was killed, Buckner had predicted that "with two dry days he could 'cut them to pieces,'" the AP reported.

Two hours before Buckner was fatally wounded, "the final assault hit its full momentum," the wire service also said. "While Adm. Chester W. Nimitz did not proclaim the campaign ended he asserted the day of Buckner's death was the day of victory." The story also quoted Nimitz's message to Buckner's troops: "x x x all of us take pride in the day of victory on which he gallantly met a soldier's death."

Buckner was buried in the Seventy-seventh Division Cemetery on Okinawa the day after he died.

> *Buckner's body was brought in a neatly made gray wooden casket to the cemetery in a field ambulance at 9 a.m. Enlisted men and officers lined the dusty road leading to the cemetery. The casket was laid against a bank of flowers on green camouflage wire as color bearers and two rifle men stood erect at the head of the casket. Geiger stood at attention with other high ranking officers of the Army, Navy and Marines during the services. The military funeral was held beneath gray skies less than 24 hours after he was killed by the enemy artillery shell which...[the aide] believes was a 75 MM.*

The *Louisville Courier-Journal* praised Buckner as a brave commander. "Under modern firepower, the general is as vulnerable as the private, and General Buckner never claimed any immunity for his rank from the dreary round of common soldiering," Graybar quoted the paper.

"Although some veterans of World War II might question the first part of the *Courier-Journal*'s statement, what was beyond doubt was Buckner's courage and his desire to see conditions at the front for himself," Graybar wrote. "These were traits he shared with his father, the first Simon Bolivar Buckner."

Disinterred in Okinawa, his remains were buried on a grassy slope below his father's grave. In 1954, Congress approved special legislation posthumously promoting Buckner to a four-star general.

Fort Buckner, a small army post on Okinawa, is named for the general. For a while, Nakagusuku Bay, which adjoins the island, was renamed Buckner Bay. In addition, Camp Bucker is a West Point training facility and Buckner Gymnasium is part of Fort Richardson, which the Kentucky-born general started at Anchorage, Alaska, in World War II.

Buckner's Hart County connection is not forgotten. He and his father are cited on a Kentucky Historical Society marker on the courthouse lawn in Munfordville. "Simon Bolivar Buckner, graduate of West Point, captain

World War II

in Mexican War, CSA general in the Civil War, governor of Kentucky, 1887–91, candidate for US Vice-President, 1896," the metal plaque reads in part. "His son S.B. Buckner, Jr., commanding general 10th US Army, killed Okinawa, 1945. Both buried in Frankfort, Ky., Cemetery."

"No Sir, I Will Not Sign"

Tuskegee Airman Roy M. Chappell was trained to fight an overseas enemy. He ended up battling racism stateside.

"What Chappell remembered most about his World War II experience was not bitterness over the racial discrimination he and his fellow officers faced, however, but his group's collective determination not to disappoint other black Americans who looked up to them," J. Todd Moye wrote in his book, *Freedom Flyers: The Tuskegee Airmen of World War II*.

Born in Williamsburg, the Whitley County seat, Chappell was one of more than one hundred African Americans arrested and officially reprimanded for refusing to agree to an unlawful order that segregated the officers' club at Freeman Field, near Seymour, Indiana, in 1945. Three were court-martialed. The incident was known as the Freeman Field Mutiny.

The Tuskegee Airmen Incorporated website says:

> *Fifty years later, on August 12, 1995, at the Tuskegee Airmen National Convention in Atlanta, Georgia, fifteen of the original one hundred and three officers that were arrested received official notification that their military records had been purged of any reference to the Freeman Field incident. Also, Mr. [Roger C.] Terry's court martial conviction had been reversed and his military record cleared. The remaining officers received instructions for clearing their records.*

Chappell, whose record was cleared, died in 2002. He was eighty-one.

He grew up in Monroe, Michigan, and lived most of his life in Chicago. But he is not forgotten in his home state.

A state historical society marker in Williamsburg commemorates his role in the Freeman Field Mutiny that, the metal plaque explains, "induced Pres. Truman to end military segregation three years later."

The Roy M. Chappell Community Education Center at Kentucky State University in Frankfort is named for him. Chappell was a junior at Kentucky State when he was drafted into the army, according to Moye.

Chappell volunteered for the army air force and trained as part of the storied Tuskegee Airmen, the country's first African American military fliers. He set out to be a pilot but ended up a navigator-bombardier with the 477th Bomb Group.

The outfit, which flew fast, twin-engine B-25 Billy Mitchell medium bombers, was supposed to ship out to the Pacific Theater. But the group was still in the United States when Japan surrendered.

While military units were segregated throughout World War II, Colonel Robert Selway's order segregating the Freeman Field officers' club violated War Department policy, Moye wrote. Selway was the base commander.

When the black flying officers were sent to Freeman Field, Selway created two officers' clubs, one for "trainee personnel" and the other for "instructor personnel." "The actual effect…was to segregate the officers' clubs on the basis of race," said Rodney A. Coleman, an assistant secretary of the air force, at the 1995 Atlanta Convention.

The newly arrived Tuskegee Airmen knew Selway's action was racist. "Everybody who was 'trainee personnel' happened to be black, and everybody that was 'instructor personnel' happened to be white," Moye quoted Chappell. "Although we had some guys back from a tour of duty overseas, all these were classified as 'trainees.'"

The African American officers—including Second Lieutenant Coleman Young, a future Detroit mayor—were determined to protest Selway's blatant discrimination against them. Several officers entered the "instructor" club in small groups. They were ordered out and arrested.

The army air force brass suggested Selway's order might have been unclear. So charges were dropped against all but three of the men, who were court-martialed. Two were acquitted; Terry, then a lieutenant, was found guilty, fined $150 and dishonorably discharged.

To make sure the black officers understood his order, Selway required each of them to read and sign it. The colonel, according to Chappell, "started calling us in one at a time, and that thing was almost like a little court martial. There were a couple of white officers, a couple of black officers, and a stenographer. And they asked us had we seen the order, had we read it?"

Chappell said he read and understood the order "but under no circumstances would he obey it," Moye wrote.

Chappell added:

> So then they read us the Sixty-Fourth Article of War, and they had one of these legal people there to explain it to us: that in time of war when you

disobey a direct order by your commanding officer you can be shot and all that kind of thing. Then the commanding officer gave us a direct order to sign the order, and I said, "No sir, I will not sign." And we were sent back to quarters under arrest.

Chappell and one hundred officers refused to sign. Rearrested, they were still under arrest when the 477th was transferred back to Godman Field at Fort Knox, Kentucky, near Louisville, on July 1. The group had gone to Freeman Field from Godman Field.

Chappell said:

And when we got back to Godman Field, they put barbed wire around the barracks and put up big poles with lights on top of them and all that shining down on us...And the strange thing was that people coming in and out of our barracks were German prisoners of war. See, they all had free range to walk all over everywhere and everything. It seemed so strange to see something like this going on. But that's what happened.

The 101 officers who would not sign the order were issued letters of reprimand charging them with "conduct unbecoming an officer, failure to obey a lawful order, and breach of good order and discipline."

After he left the army air force, Chappell earned a bachelor's degree at Roosevelt University in Chicago. He was a teacher and guidance counselor in city schools and also a post office supervisor. In addition, Chappell was president of the Chicago chapter of the Tuskegee Airmen veterans group.

Upon his death, the Illinois House of Representatives approved a resolution mourning "the passing of Roy M. Chappell." It also said "the Freeman Field Mutiny is widely credited with creating the pressure that eventually ended all official racial discrimination in the military."

"We Couldn't Understand Him at First Because He Was from Brooklyn"

Maxine Bohannon figured the knock at her door early that hot summer morning was a neighbor.

"So we just said, 'Come in,'" she remembered. "There was this man standing there holding a parachute. His face was kind of bloody. We'd never seen him before."

B-29 monument.
Courtesy of the author.

The stranger was Corporal Irving A. Elias, sole survivor of an all-but-forgotten crash of a B-29 bomber close to Benton, the Marshall County seat, in World War II. "We couldn't understand him at first because he was from Brooklyn," Bohannon said.

She still lives near where the big, four-engine warplane went down in a fierce thunderstorm around 1:00 a.m. on July 1, 1945. The crash site is near Soldier Creek Church.

A stone memorial marks the spot. An inscription on the slab says it was erected "IN REMEMBRANCE OF THEIR SACRIFICE AND OF THOSE WHO HAVE SERVED AND CONTINUE TO SERVE ON FOREIGN AND DOMESTIC SOILS AS AMBASSADORS FOR OUR FREEDOM AND DEMOCRACY."

World War II

Four officers and six enlisted men were aboard the silvery Superfortress that "seemed to disintegrate" in flight, Elias told the *Benton Tribune-Democrat*. Only he managed to parachute to safety.

The wreckage was scattered "over a two-mile area," the paper reported. "The bodies of the four officers and five enlisted men, badly mangled, were in two separate groups."

Bohannon said her late husband, Ernest Bohannon, drove Elias to a hospital in nearby Mayfield. "Except for lacerations of the face, hands and feet, he was unhurt," the *Tribune-Democrat* said.

Elias, the plane's left waist gunner, told the newspaper that "they were flying through a severe electrical storm and heavy rain when there was a loud explosion."

The aviator said he "had just left his post and was in the tail of the plane" when the B-29 broke up, according to the *Tribune-Democrat*. "He recalled being thrown clear, opening his parachute, and falling about 8,000 feet," the paper added. "Elias said it was pitch dark when he landed in a field and the rain was descending in torrents."

The flier crawled under a bush, where he stayed until daybreak. He walked a short distance to the Bohannon house.

"Thousands of people viewed the wreckage...before Army officials arrived and placed guards on the scene," the *Tribune-Democrat* said. "The whole neighborhood went to see it," Bohannon recalled. "But I didn't look at the bodies."

The B-29 was based at Kirtland Army Airfield in Albuquerque, New Mexico, and was on a routine flight, the paper said. The ill-fated bomber refueled in Nashville shortly before it was lost.

The bodies of the dead airmen were taken to the Camp Campbell army base near Clarksville, Tennessee.

"We didn't hear the plane crash," Bohannon said. "Most of the wreckage was near the Soldier Creek Church, but there were parts of the plane all over. The motors fell in different places."

The debris was cleared from woods and farm fields soon after the crash. But relic hunters, probing with metal detectors, still occasionally unearth bits of the bomber's aluminum skin and other small parts.

The B-29 was the largest and most powerful U.S. bomber of World War II. Massed B-29s flew many air raids against Japan and dropped the atomic bombs on Hiroshima and Nagasaki that ended the war in August 1945.

"SUBJECT: Birthday Cake"

Petty Officer Billy Hagan, U.S. Navy, took a break from battling the Japanese in the Philippines to unwrap a box of homemade Christmas candy from his mom.

"By the time he got it, the candy had gone bad," Zach Hagan said. "So my great-grandmother, Kathaleen Hagan, sent a letter to President Harry Truman. She asked him to see to it that Billy got a birthday cake instead."

Hagan had his cake and ate it, too, thanks to his commander in chief.

Billy and Kathaleen Hagan, both deceased, were from Fulton, about as far west as Kentucky goes. Zach Hagan lives near Paducah, the McCracken County seat, with his father, Richard Hagan, Billy's son.

The Hagans cherish the copy of the letter to Truman. Kathaleen Hagan wrote it on September 2, 1945, the day Japan formally surrendered and officially ended World War II.

The family also has a duplicate of a Navy Department memo to Hagan's skipper asking "that the wishes of the boy's mother be complied with, if practicable."

Billy Hagan was proud of the cake, according to his grandson. "But his shipmates ragged him so much about it that he asked his mother never to write the president again."

Kathaleen Hagan told Truman she mailed her two sons candy for Christmas in 1944. Billy's big brother, James Howard Hagan, also of Fulton, was in the army, fighting the Germans in Europe.

"I worked hard and used most of our sugar," she explained. "The older boy received his O.K. but the one in the Pacific did not get anything that was eatable when it reached him sometime in February and I mailed the packages on October 15th."

Hagan was aboard LST—Landing Ship, Tank—number 666. His ship won six battle stars in the Pacific Theater in 1944–1945.

"September 30th 1945 will be his second birthday aboard this LST," Kathaleen Hagan informed the president. "He will be 20 years old. I am going to ask you to see he has a cake made for him on that day with 20 candles on it, large enough for all his buddies."

Truman, or one of his aides, passed Hagan's letter to the Navy Bureau of Supplies and Accounts in Washington. E.F. Ney, bureau chief, contacted Hagan's captain.

"Subject: Birthday cake," read Ney's memo of September 17, 1945. "Reference: Ltr. of Mrs. J.L. Hagan of Fulton, Kentucky…to the President."

World War II

Hagan confessed to Truman that her sons "never knew what it was to be away until this terrible war started. I have prayed so much for their safety and a speedy return home."

She promised the president, "I shall never forget you for this kind act and too I know Billy will be grateful for having received a nice cake on his birthday from mother and being so far from home and loved ones, and so young when he had to leave."

Kentucky's Sole Triple-Admiral Town?

Paducah might be Kentucky's only three-admiral town.

Joe Clifton, Eugene Paro Sr. and William O. Burch Jr. hailed from the McCracken County seat. All three were decorated World War II heroes who earned flag rank in the U.S. Navy.

Clifton. *Courtesy of the Market House Museum.*

Paro. *Courtesy of Colonel Eugene Paro Jr., USMC, retired.*

"They're not very well known in Paducah," said historian and author John E.L. Robertson Sr. "But they should be."

Paducah's Joe Clifton Drive is named for the rear admiral dubbed "Jumping Joe." Neither Burch nor Paro—also rear admirals—has been so honored.

"Joseph Clinton Clifton was born in Marion, Kentucky, October 31, 1908," Robertson wrote in *Profiles of Paducah People*, a book he coauthored with Allan Rhodes Sr. "He died December 24, 1967. In between, he became a legend among many, especially U.S. Navy fliers."

Robertson quoted from *My Paducah: From the Early Years to the Present* by Barron White, who wrote that Clifton "logged more than 10,000 hours in propeller and jet aircraft. His group inflicted this damage on the Japanese: 102 planes destroyed, 78 planes damaged, 104,500 tons of shipping sunk and 198,500 tons of shipping damaged."

World War II

White added that Clifton earned the Legion of Merit with Gold Star, the Distinguished Flying Cross with Gold Star, a pair of Air Medals and a British Distinguished Service Order. Robertson wrote that Clifton shot down five enemy planes to become an ace while he was serving aboard the USS *Saratoga*, an aircraft carrier, early in the war. He ended the war as executive officer of another carrier, the USS *Wasp*.

When he was a boy, Clifton moved with his family to Paducah and graduated from Augusta Tilghman High School. He starred on the football team, according to Robertson and White.

He earned his "Jumping Joe" monicker during a fateful football game, according to records in the city's Market House Museum:

> *Joe, as a defensive* [back]…*came up repeatedly against a big Tennessee player. Time and time again, a wiry (sometimes called scrawny) Joe made the Herculean effort to gain possession of the ball. Once, two guards caught Clifton and carried him backwards by the arms, twenty yards! Joe watched attentively for the big guard to make a wrong maneuver. Then the opportunity Clifton was waiting for, came. The guard fumbled the ball, and Joe grabbed it and ran, jumping through the astonished guards as he flew to make a 73 yard touchdown…He was to become the idol of girls in every soda fountain in Paducah.*

After attending the University of Kentucky for a year, he transferred to the U.S. Naval Academy, where he graduated in 1930 and was commissioned an ensign. He played football at the academy. He was named an All Eastern Conference fullback and earned All American honorable mention.

Clifton won the coveted gold wings of a naval aviator in 1932. Ten years later, he took command of the *Saratoga*'s Fighter Squadron Twelve

Clifton and his pilots flew F4U Corsair and F6F fighters against the Japanese. Once, he got a rare opportunity to pilot an enemy plane: a captured Zero fighter. The navy devised new dogfighting tactics based on his evaluation of the Zero.

In 1944, Clifton was promoted to commander of Air Group Twelve, which combined warplanes from the *Saratoga* and HMS *Illustrious*, a British flattop. After battling the Japanese, the *Saratoga* returned stateside, where a *Time* magazine reporter caught up with Clifton and his fliers:

> *By their own account, there was not a hero among them.*
> *The outfit itself was the hero, and one of the greatest turned out yet by the Navy. Its skipper, Commander Joseph Clinton Clifton, a 36-year-old*

precision product of Annapolis and Pensacola, had seen to that. Sinewy "Jumping Joe," who was never known to sit in a chair more than 30 seconds at a time, had put the group straight on his views right from the start. They were a team; there was no room for hot-shots or prima donnas no time for the slightest bit of sloppy flying, bad shooting, lazy tactics.

Time also reported that Clifton, who suffered a banged-up nose from "'backing up a weak line at Annapolis,' indulged in a few periods of silence during that 15 months. But they were mostly when he was in his bunk. In battle and out, he kept up a rapid fire of instruction, reprimand [and] occasional praise. Group Twelve responded to his coaching: the score showed it."

Clifton's group lost only a dozen planes to the Japanese. Three fliers were killed in action, and another twenty were missing, according to *Time*. But they gave more than they got.

Group Twelve

destroyed 102 enemy planes, sank 104,500 tons of shipping, damaged 198,500 tons more. It fought land-based in the Solomons for a week, averaged around five hours a day of fighting for every crew, and lost not one aircraft.

Carrier-based again, Air Group Twelve smashed at Rabaul, fought in the Gilbert Islands (Tarawa) invasion, roved the Marshalls for 25 days, blasted the way for U.S. landings in Eniwetok in the Navy's knifing attack across the Pacific. Then it swung far to the southwest, joined up with British forces in Trincomalee, Ceylon.

Teaming with the British, and Clifton commanding the combined air groups,

Group Twelve slashed at Jap[anese] *bases at Sabang on the tip of Sumatra and the once-great Dutch naval base at Surabaya. Group Twelve lost one plane in each show.*

Joe Clifton saw his wingman, "Klondike," with whom he had flown close to 500 hours, go down at sea. "He must be saved!" Joe bellowed over the radio. He gathered his Hellcats to smash at shore-based artillery and beat it down until Klondike (Lieut. (j.g.) Dale Klahn) was picked up by a British submarine in a hair-raising rescue.

World War II

Time said Group Twelve was to be disbanded "to spread their lore among new airmen." Clifton's fliers "carried away many another memory last week as they said goodbye and went to their new stations. But none was sharper than the great carrier strike on Rabaul on Nov. 5, 1943."

The attack was the group's biggest show to that point in the war, according to *Time*.

> *The outfit (said Joe) was "scared—but not afraid." By Admiral Halsey's order they were to help beat down a Jap[anese] task force, keep it from moving south and smashing inferior U.S. naval forces in the Solomons. There could be no failures by Group Twelve.*
>
> *The helmeted pilots sat in the ready-room and waited. They had been briefed. For once, Jumping Joe ran out of conversation. Finally he got out his Testament and began to read aloud the gist Psalm:*
>
> *"He that dwelleth in the secret place of the most High shall abide under the shadow of the Almighty. I will say of the Lord, He is my refuge and my fortress…Surely He shall deliver thee from the snare of the fowler…For He shall give His angels charge over thee."*
>
> *The call came: "Pilots, man your planes!" Group Twelve went out to battle, and won.*

Advanced rear admiral after the war, Clifton spent most of the rest of his career in charge of various pilot training facilities, including the big naval air station at Millington, near Memphis.

"Joe kept in such good shape that when he took command at NAS Memphis, 1954–56, he actually played in a football game, wearing his favorite number 35," Robertson wrote. "Despite his 47 years, Clifton gained 30 yards and made four solo tackles!"

Robertson added that many of Clifton's student pilots knew him as "Whispering Joe." It was a joke. If they needed dressing down, Clifton could yell loud enough "to drown out a row of planes" with their engines running, according to Robertson.

Other students, the author added, "recall his tailored uniforms and his insisting on two scoops of ice cream on his cereal; others note that he used cologne but would fight any who questioned it."

Clifton died in 1967 at age sixty-six and was buried in Arlington National Cemetery. "How sad was his end," Robertson wrote. "The great athlete had circulation problems and both legs and a kidney were removed before he died."

A year after his death, the navy authorized the Joseph C. Clifton trophy. The award honors meritorious achievement by a fighter squadron flying off an aircraft carrier.

Like Clifton, Paro—born in Paducah in 1904—was a standout high school football player. He was the team captain.

Paro graduated from the naval academy in 1925 and spent the early part of his career mostly in the Far East before graduating from submarine school at New London, Connecticut, in 1928.

When the war began, Lieutenant Commander Paro was an engineering officer aboard the USS *Canopus*, a submarine tender, in the Philippines. After the Japanese invaded the strategic islands, Paro supervised the scuttling of the ship in Mariveles Bay to keep the enemy from getting it.

The Philippines fell in May 1942. Most of the American defenders and many of their Filipino allies were killed or captured. Paro was gravely wounded but was evacuated.

On October 9, 1942, the *Sun-Democrat* published a letter Paro wrote to his mother, telling her about his battles with the Japanese. The letter and a photo of the officer were printed on page one:

> *Christmas Day, when Manila was about to fall, I received orders to take a convoy of trucks and a battalion of men consisting of blue jackets and stragglers and try to get to Bataan.*
>
> *Under constant bombardment from the air by the Jap[anese]...we finally came to a stream 100 feet wide; we had to build a bridge for the trucks to cross; we had one ax and half a keg of nails; we worked all day, crossed the bridge and entrenched ourselves on the other side. The Jap[anese]... arrived, took the bridge and attacked us. Bombs fell all around us; one within 15 feet of the foxhole I was in. We were two weeks making our way to Bataan, fighting all the way, living on dry rice and salmon.*
>
> *Arriving in Bataan, I was placed in charge of a battalion of men on the coast with machine guns.*

From Bataan, Paro and his men were sent to Corregidor Island, where he earned a Silver Star. According to the citation that came with the medal, Paro displayed

> *conspicuous gallantry and intrepidity in action against the enemy while attached to the Submarine Detachment...Though subjected to almost continuous enemy aerial attack, Commander Paro risked his life on*

World War II

numerous occasions to carry out vital missions during the prolonged siege of Corregidor and the subsequent evacuation of personnel from that hazardous area. Cool and remarkably resourceful in spite of constant danger, and working under great difficulties caused by lack of equipment, he contributed immeasurably to the uninterrupted operations of various units and to the heroic defense of Corregidor.

Corregidor was a fortress built to guard the entrance to Manila Bay. Dubbed the Rock, the strongpoint bristled with long-range guns and was honeycombed with tunnels for sheltering troops and storing ammunition and supplies. Paro was near a tunnel entrance when a one-thousand-pound Japanese bomb exploded just outside.

The blast ripped off Paro's clothes and knocked him fifty feet deeper in the tunnel, according to Colonel Eugene E. Paro Jr., U.S. Marine Corps, retired, of Huntsville, Alabama. The western Kentuckian suffered severe blood clots in both temples, but he "was still functioning," his son said.

On February 3, 1942, Paro left Corregidor aboard the USS *Trout*, a submarine loaded with unusual ballast: twenty tons of gold bars and silver pesos—the Filipino treasury. The *Trout* had arrived with 3,500 rounds of three-inch antiaircraft ammunition.

After the welcome cargo was unloaded, the *Trout* was found to be too light to dive. Neither concrete sacks nor sandbags were handy.

The Filipino government did not want its treasury to fall into enemy hands. "So the gold bullion was used as ballast," Colonel Paro said.

Lieutenant Commander Paro was considered too valuable to leave behind, too. "At that time the navy had an acoustic homing torpedo that was in the developmental stages," Paro said. "My father was privy to information about it. The navy was afraid if the Japanese captured him, they would torture the information out of him. So he was evacuated on the *Trout*."

The senior Paro ultimately wound up in Australia. He seemed to be overcoming his injuries when he lost consciousness boarding a warship. "He fell off the gangway between the ship and the pier," Colonel Paro said.

His father was dispatched to a naval hospital in Oakland, California, where surgeons removed the clots and inserted a protective metal plate on one side of his head. Afterward, he returned home and was interviewed by a *Sun-Democrat* reporter. An undated clipping of the story is in the McCracken County Public Library.

Paro survived the bombing of Manila, the Philippine capital, according to the newspaper. He "witnessed the destruction of fuel tanks, flying fields and other material. He was in on the city's evacuation and took command of a fleet of trucks down Bataan Peninsula. He was also in charge of servicing the submarines used in running the Nippon blockade."

Paro said "the last days of Bataan were a taste of hell, beyond the imagination of a human being, with the Army blowing up ammunition dumps, all roads filled with military traffic and hectic rescue work going on under Jap[anese] fire."

Paro said engineers blew up the USS *Dewey*, a floating dry dock, to keep it from the Japanese. They also used explosives to seal both ends of "a tunnel built to protect stored fuel oil and gas," he told the *Sun-Democrat*.

He added:

> *A short time later the whole mountain under which the tunnel was dug erupted in a tremendous blast. The explosion hurled rocks for a radius of two miles destroying practically every small craft in the harbor and inflicting heavy casualties on the personnel…The entire operation was a race against time in order to have it completed before morning and arrival of Nippon dive bombers.*

The article additionally quoted Paro:

> *There were untold numbers of heroic acts that night, but most of them will never be recorded. Many of the heroes died before the night passed and their deeds were lost in the hell of hectic struggle for life.*
>
> *Actual departure from Corregidor necessitated a dangerous exit from the harbor…Our craft* [a minesweeper] *had to pass within 300 yards of the Japanese artillery, which had been raining shells on the fortress all day, due to proximity of our own mine field.*

Paro got away, but it was a close call for the Kentuckian. After the minesweeper ran "the battery gauntlet," the little ship "was illuminated by searchlights from three Jap[anese] destroyers," the paper said.

"We made it when the threat of gunfire from Corregidor caused them to withdraw," Paro said. "We continued to a submarine with which we were to make contact and reached comparative safety with our cargo of men from the doomed fortress."

The article said Paro "was in command of the [detachment]…which loaded the Philippine bullion aboard [the *Trout*]…and personally handled most of it…He assisted in evacuation of the Philippine high commissioner and President Manuel Quezon."

World War II

In the article, Paro urged civilians to do their part to help defeat the enemy. "People here in the United States don't realize how small things can help win the war, although optimism is dawning within our armed forces the need for complete civilian cooperation is greater now than ever."

He conceded "it is difficult to conceive that slow driving, conservation of fuel oil, gasoline and other sacrifices Americans have been asked to make really save the lives of youngsters out there in the thick of things," the paper said.

Paro also said:

> *But it's true, and when that point of realization is reached the kind of civilian cooperation necessary for victory is at hand...I visited Japan nearly a year before Pearl Harbor and taxi cabs (there were no pleasure autos) were limited to two gallons of gas a day and buildings had already been stripped of their iron work.*
>
> *That was a year before war started. The Japanese are...determined... people and their fighting forces have the unified and solid support of the entire nation.*

Paro recovered and returned to duty, eventually commanding submarine-hunting destroyer escorts in the Caribbean. One of his officers was Franklin D. Roosevelt Jr.

Paro went back to the Pacific Theater and landed with army and marine troops on Okinawa in April 1945. Part of Buckner's staff, he was wounded again.

After the war, Paro was promoted to rear admiral. Following his retirement from the navy in 1949, he returned to his hometown and became a painter and sculptor. "Besides having a successful one-man show at the Feragil Gallery in New York, he sculpted a bronze bust of Vice President Alben Barkley, displayed at Barkley Dam," according to his obituary in the *Paducah Sun*. The admiral also "painted a mural of early American life for the [old] Paducah Post Office [now the federal court building]."

Paro died in Huntsville in 1990 and was buried in Arlington National Cemetery. The admiral was eighty-six years old.

Burch must have crossed paths with Paro at Annapolis. After graduating from Tilghman High School, he enrolled in the naval academy in 1923 and graduated four years later. Like Clifton, he opted for naval aviation and earned his pilot's wings in 1930. "During the war Burch served as commander of Scouting Squadron 5" in the Pacific Theater, Robertson wrote. A lieutenant commander, he was based on the carrier USS *Yorktown*.

On January 21, 1942, Burch and his fliers took part in some of the earliest U.S. offensive operations against the Japanese—air raids on enemy positions in the Marshall and Gilbert Islands. He led an attack by nine SBD Dauntless dive bombers against Makin and Mili Atolls in the Gilberts, according to *Black Shoe Carrier Admiral: Frank Jack Fletcher at Coral Sea, Midway and Guadalcanal*, by John B. Lundstrom. "He personally 'made direct bomb hits on an enemy seaplane tender and sank a four-engine patrol plane on the water by machine gun fire,'" Robertson wrote. "For this action, he received the Distinguished Flying Cross."

On March 10, planes from the *Yorktown* raided Salamaua and Lae in the Coral Sea. "It was almost a duplicate of, and even more successful than, the Makin attack, except that the pilots were warned about forced landings in the jungles where there were head-hunters," according to a story by John Field in the November 16, 1942 issue of *Life* magazine.

He quoted Burch: "Our torpedo bombers made successful level bombing attacks. Our fighters shot down two [Japanese] seaplanes and strafed both surface ships and ground installations. Our dive bombers sank cargo ships and destroyers. All told, the operation completely wiped the place out."

In May 1942, the *Yorktown* helped stop a Japanese drive toward Australia by fighting the enemy to a standstill in the Battle of the Coral Sea. The next month, Burch saw action in the Battle of Midway, a signal American victory that turned the tide of war against the Japanese.

But at Midway, the Japanese got even with the *Yorktown*. They sank the carrier, while losing four carriers of their own.

Burch earned the Navy Cross—second only to the Medal of Honor—three times. He earned his first one at Tulagi in the Solomon Islands, where he again led Scouting Squadron 5 in harm's way on May 4. The Japanese "apparently…made the mistake of putting part of their fleet into port," Field wrote.

He quoted Burch once more:

> *All I could see in the harbor were three cargo ships. We started down. As I approached I saw a large heavy cruiser off to the side, under a cloud; tied up alongside it was a lighter cruiser and a destroyer. The torpedo squadron, as they approached, could see much better than we could. All the ships had a few bombs dropped on them. You could see the torpedoes and bombs hitting, and the nest of three ships was knocked apart.*
>
> *We went back to the ship to get more bombs. I told them we had hit the [Japanese]…but wanted to go back….They said "go back."*

World War II

We returned with our second load. Just outside Tulagi harbor, a heavy cruiser was underway. We made an attack on her. We went in against the cruiser alone and made two bomb hits.

Robertson quoted from Burch's Navy Cross citation:

Due to Lieutenant Commander Burch's distinguished and capable leadership, the high combat efficiency attained by units under his command enabled them to deliver five aggressive and exceptionally successful dive-bombing attacks, the first at Tulagi Harbor…in which at least eight enemy Japanese vessels were destroyed or severely damaged, and later on May 7, when an enemy carrier was sunk.

(The carrier was the *Shokaku*, which was severely damaged but repaired. A U.S. submarine sank the carrier in 1943.)

Burch's bravery and skill "contributed materially to the success of our forces in the Battle of the Coral Sea," the citation also said.

Also in 1942, Burch earned a gold star for his Navy Cross—signifying a second decoration. His citation said he "fearlessly leading his squadron over high mountains and dense jungles of New Guinea in a dive-bombing attack against three enemy airplane tenders or transports…He and his squadron scored seven direct hits and eight very near misses against the hostile vessels, one direct hit being made by Lieutenant Commander Burch personally." Burch "contributed materially to the sinking of the three Japanese ships."

Later, Burch was promoted to executive officer of the aircraft carrier USS *Ticonderoga*. "Here he earned his Gold Star in lieu of this third Navy Cross by directing the fire detail dealing with a suicide bomber that crashed into his ship," Robertson wrote.

Two kamikaze planes struck the *Ticonderoga* in the South China Sea off Fomosa on January 21, 1945, heavily damaging the warship. Burch's citation read:

Organizing fire-fighting crews on the hangar deck after his ship had been hit, Burch was the first to take a hose into the fire despite the billowing flames and continuous ammunition explosions although his clothes caught fire on two occasions. After the fire-fighting crews were functioning, he made his way to secondary control and manned his exposed battle station until severely wounded by shrapnel. Refusing to go to Sick Bay, he gave orders to be carried to the flight deck where he directed the fire fighting until the flames were under control. *His conduct throughout was in keeping with the highest traditions of the Navy of the United States.*

Promoted to rear admiral on July 1, 1945, Burch retired from the navy in 1962. In 1989, he died at Virginia Beach, Virginia, where he is buried.

"We Suffered under Nazi Occupation for Four Years"

The number 2680 could have added up to torture and death for "Bernadette."

"That was my number and my name in the French resistance," said Jeanine Caubit Williams of Paducah. "I hate Hitler and the Nazis. We must never forget the Holocaust. But I don't hate the German people because I am a Christian."

Williams, who has since died, married an American soldier. The couple ended up in Paducah.

Williams was nineteen in the spring of 1940 when German soldiers invaded Belgium and then swept into France. The Caubit family lived near Paris.

"We saw the refugees, multitudes of them from Belgium, on the road walking, riding whatever they had to take them somewhere else," she said. "That happened almost right under our windows. We were facing a large main road. We realized that things were getting really bad."

Before Paris fell to the German army, her father, a government employee, was ordered to Orleans, about seventy-five miles away.

> *We had the impression that we would have transportation, but were told to go by our own means. That meant our legs.*
>
> *We lived in a beautiful suburb twelve miles west of Paris. We didn't want to go, but they told us we had to because the bridges were going to be blown up.*

Williams, her ten-year-old sister, their parents and her father's mother all left on foot. "We were on the road for one week, but it seemed like one year."

She said her seventy-eight-year-old grandmother was witnessing her third war and third German invasion. She was a teen during the Franco-Prussian War. Four of her sons fought the enemy in World War I.

"They were all at the front," Williams said. "My father was badly wounded. Two of his brothers were gassed. One survived and the other died just after the war. The other brother was missing in action and never found."

World War II

The Caubits joined a flood of refugees walking, pedaling bicycles or riding in cars, trucks and horse-drawn farm wagons. Here and there in the tired procession were retreating French troops. "They were regrouping south of Paris."

Food and water were scarce for soldiers and civilians. "We went into the fields and ate dirty lettuce and little green peas," Williams said. "We tried to find something to eat in any store that had any food to sell. We got some water from the fountains in the village squares."

She said people in the villages through which they passed "spread some hay and straw in the outbuildings for us to sleep on. The first night, we slept on top of some cement bags."

She said about midway to Orleans, German and Italian warplanes bombed and strafed the ragged column. In the panic and confusion, Williams and her grandmother got separated from the rest of the family.

"The Italians dove so low on us you could almost see the whites of their eyes," Williams said. "This was our aimless exodus."

Some French soldiers gave her and her grandmother a lift in an army truck and then dropped them off in a village. "We just sat down and cried," Williams said. "We didn't think we'd see the family again."

But her father found them after a daylong search. "It was pure luck," Williams said. "No, it was God."

She and her grandmother were luckier than they knew. Williams said that, the next day, the reunited Caubits passed the wreckage of a truck that looked familiar to her grandmother and to her. "It was the one we were on. The truck was blown up, and all the friendly soldiers were dead."

Later, German troops caught up with the refugees and stopped them. They marched French troops off to prisoner of war camps and ordered the civilians to go home.

"The Nazis were in heavy trucks. Each had a machine gun pointed at us. This you never forget no matter how long you live."

Williams said she did not know how far the family had walked. "But we went back home, past abandoned French tanks with 'out of gas' chalked on them, past empty cars, the fresh graves of French soldiers on the roadside and dead horses swelled up like big balloons. Trash was everywhere. It was a mess too horrible to describe."

Officially, Williams volunteered for the resistance in 1942. "But I became a resister in my heart on the way home."

She said her first act of resistance was helping some French POWs. "We had been resting for a while next to a fountain in front of the church. The fountain was dry. Here came the prisoners with their German guards. They all rushed for the fountain to get some water.

"I told mom, 'Let's get them some water.' We borrowed their canteens and got some water for them from a faucet behind the church. The Germans didn't like it. But they didn't stop us."

As a resistance fighter, Williams risked her life many times. She spread news by secretly listening to Allied radio broadcasts from London. She passed out anti-Nazi leaflets. "All we got from the Germans was propaganda. It was forbidden to listen to Allied Broadcasts.

"Allied planes would drop the leaflets at night. I'd sneak out, gather them up and take them to Paris and give them away. If the Nazis had caught me, I'd have been shot."

Bernadette took a job at Printemps, the popular Paris department store. "Some Jews secretly made clothes for us and we had a spy in the store, a woman, who wrote their names down and was planning to turn them in," she said.

Williams and a coworker got the woman's purse and tore up the list. Her cover blown, the spy disappeared. "The next day, the streets were full of German soldiers. I don't know if they were looking for us or what. It was frightening, but they let us go."

After Allied armies liberated France in 1944, Williams joined the Free French Air Force and earned sergeant's stripes. She wed Corporal Charles Williams in 1946. "I went from Paris, France, to Paris, Tennessee, where his family was from," she said chuckling. "Then we came to Paducah."

Williams treasured the gold wings she wore on her air force cap and her resistance armband. The old white cloth was marked with the red, white and blue colors of France, the Cross of Lorraine and her resistance number.

She also prized a stack of old French coins, each one minted with a hole in the middle. Knotted twine held the coins together.

"The Germans tried to get all the coins like these because they are made of nickel," she said. "They wanted to melt them down to make weapons. They told us on the radio from London to save the coins. I put mine on a little string.

"We suffered under Nazi occupation for four years. Every day, I saw the Germans in my country with their big guns and their tanks. I heard the noisy clack of their boots on the streets and listened to their war songs."

Bibliography

Belue, Ted Franklin, ed. *A Sketch of the Life and Character of Daniel Boone: A Memoir by Peter Houston.* Mechanicsburg, PA: Stackpole Books, 1997.
Benton Tribune-Democrat.
Blatt, Heiman. *Sons of Men: Evansville's War Record.* Evansville, IN: Abe P. Madison, 1920.
Bodley, Temple, and Samuel M. Wilson. *History of Kentucky.* Chicago: Charles Kerr Publishers, 1928.
Boller, Paul F., Jr. *Presidential Anecdotes.* New York: Oxford University Press, 1981.
———. *Presidential Campaigns.* New York: Oxford University Press, 1984.
Brininstool, E.A. *Troopers with Custer: Historic Incidents of the Battle of the Little Big Horn.* Lincoln: University of Nebraska Press, 1952.
"Canada Within the Empire: Confederation and Expansion 1867–1870." WarMuseum.ca, http://www.warmuseum.ca/cwm/exhibitions/chrono/1774confederation_e.shtml (accessed December 14, 2010).
Carleton, Captain James Henry. *The Battle of Buena Vista with the Operations of the "Army of Occupation" for One Month.* New York: Harper and Brothers, 1848.
Caudill, Harry M. *The Mountain, the Miner and the Lord.* Lexington: University Press of Kentucky, 1980.
Cecil, Jerry. "Lieutenant Crittenden: Striving for the Soldier's Life." *Greasy Grass* no. 11 (1995).

BIBLIOGRAPHY

Cobb, Irvin S. *Exit Laughing*. Indianapolis, IN: Bobbs-Merrill Company, 1941.

Collins, Lewis. *Historical Sketches of Kentucky*. Maysville, KY, and Cincinnati, KY: Lewis Collins and J.A. & U.P. James, 1850.

Collins, Lewis, and Richard Collins. *A History of Kentucky*. Covington, KY: Collins and Company, 1882.

Custer, Elizabeth. *Boots and Saddles, or Life in Dakota with General Custer*. New York and London: Harper Brothers Publishers, 1899.

Draper, Lyman C., and Ted Franklin Belue, eds. *The Life of Daniel Boone*. Mechanicsburg, PA: Stackpole Books, 1998.

Evansville Courier.

Faragher, John Mack. *Daniel Boone: The Life and Legend of an American Pioneer*. New York: Henry Holt and Company, 1992.

Franklin, John Hope. *From Slavery to Freedom: A History of American Negroes*. New York: Alfred A. Knopf, 1947.

Graybar, Lloyd J. "The Buckners of Kentucky." *Filson Club History Quarterly* 58 (April 1984).

Harrison, Lowell H., and James C. Klotter. *A New History of Kentucky*. Lexington: University Press of Kentucky, 1997.

Henderson Gleaner.

Hoehling, A.A. *The Fierce Lambs*. Boston: Little, Brown and Co., 1960.

Indiana World War Records: Gold Star Honor Roll, A Record of Indiana Men and Women Who Died in the Service of the United States and the Allied Nations in the World War, 1914–1918. Indianapolis: Indiana Historical Commission, 1921.

Jablonski, Edward. *Flying Fortress: The Illustrated History of the B-17s and the Men Who Flew Them*. New York: Doubleday, 1965.

Jones, Richard Seelye. *A History of the American Legion*. Indianapolis, IN: Bobbs-Merrill Company, 1946.

"King, Amon Butler" (1807–1836). The Handbook of Texas Online. http://www.tshaonline.org/handbook/online/articles/KK/fki15.html (accessed December 14, 2010).

Kleber, John E. *The Kentucky Encyclopedia*. Lexington: University Press of Kentucky, 1992.

Lawson, Anita. *Irvin S. Cobb*. Bowling Green, OH: Bowling Green State University Popular Press, 1984.

Lexington Daily Press.

Life.

Lord, Walter. *Day of Infamy*. New York: Holt, Rhinehart and Winston, 1957.

Lundstrom, John B. *Black Shoe Carrier Admiral: Frank Jack Fletcher at Coral Sea, Midway and Guadalcanal*. Annapolis, MD: Naval Institute Press, 2006.

Bibliography

MacDonald, Charles B. *The Mighty Endeavor: American Armed Forces in the European Theater in World War II.* New York: Oxford University Press, 1969.

Marshall, S.L.A. *The American Heritage History of World War I.* New York: American Heritage-Bonanza Books, 1982.

McClure, Daniel Elmo, Jr. *Two Centuries in Elizabethtown and Hardin County, Kentucky.* Elizabethtown, KY: Hardin County Historical Society, 1999.

McMaster, John B. *The United States in the World War 1918–1920.* New York: D. Appleton and Co., 1920.

Moye, J. Todd. *Freedom Flyers: The Tuskegee Airmen of World War II.* New York: Oxford University Press, 2010.

Oliver, John W., ed. *Gold Star Honor Roll: A Record of Indiana Men and Women Who Died in Service of the United States and the Allied Nations in the World War, 1914–1918.* Indianapolis: Indiana Historical Commission, 1921.

Owensboro Messenger-Inquirer.

Paducah Sun.

Paducah Sun-Democrat.

"Refugio, Battle of." The Handbook of Texas Online, http://www.tshaonline.org/handbook/online/articles/qer01 (accessed December 14, 2010).

Remini, Robert. *Henry Clay: Statesman for the Union.* New York: W.W. Norton & Company, 1991.

Robertson, James M. "Captain Amon B. King." *Southwestern Historical Quarterly* 29 (October 1925).

Robertson, John E.L., Sr., and Allan Rhodes Sr. *Profiles of Paducah People.* Paducah, KY: Image Graphics, 2008.

Rothert, Otto A. *History of Muhlenberg County.* Louisville, KY: J.P. Morton & Company, 1913.

Schurz, Karl. *Life of Henry Clay: American Statesman.* Boston and New York: Houghton, Mifflin and Company, 1887.

Simkins, Francis Butler, and Charles P. Roland. *A History of the South.* 3rd ed. New York: Alfred A. Knopf, 1967.

Smith, Charles E. *The Honor Roll of McCracken County: An Illustrated Historical Biography Compiled from Private Records as Furnished by the Individuals, Relatives and Friends of Those Illustrated in this Volume.* Paducah, KY: Billings Printing Company, 1919.

Smith, Z.F. *The History of Kentucky.* Louisville, KY: Prentice Press, 1895.

Sterling, Forrest J. *Wake of the Wahoo.* Philadelphia, PA: Chilton Company, 1960.

Bibliography

Thompson, George Raynor, and Dixie R Harris. *The Signal Corps: The Outcome (Mid-1943 through 1945), U.S. Army in World War II*. Washington, D.C.: Center for Military History, 1966.

"351st Bomb Group, 1943–1945, Polebrook, Northamptonshire, England: Group History." 351st BG, http://351st.org/ken.harbour/ (accessed December 14, 2010).

Time.

Werstein, Irving. *The Battle of Aachen*. New York: Thomas Y. Crowell, 1962.

Whitaker, Fess. *History of Corporal Fess Whitaker*. Louisville, KY: Standard Printing Company, 1918.

"Who were the Tuskegee Airmen?" Tuskegee Airmen, Inc. http://www.tuskegeeairmen.org/Tuskegee_Airmen_History.html (accessed December 18, 2010).

About the Author

Berry Craig is a professor of history at West Kentucky Community and Technical College in Paducah. A former daily newspaper feature writer and columnist, he is also a freelance journalist and author. Craig wrote *True Tales of Old-Time Kentucky Politics: Bombast, Bourbon and Burgoo* and *Hidden History of Kentucky in the Civil War*, both from The History Press. Craig is a native of Mayfield, Kentucky, where he lives with his wife and their teenage son.

Visit us at
www.historypress.net

www.ingramcontent.com/pod-product-compliance
Lightning Source LLC
Chambersburg PA
CBHW042142160426
43201CB00022B/2378